INFORMATION SCIENCE:
Information, Knowledge, Communication and Libraries

INFORMATION SCIENCE:
Information, Knowledge, Communication and Libraries

By

PROF. C. A. AUGUSTINE

Ess Ess Publications
New Delhi

INFORMATION SCIENCE:
Information, Knowledge, Communication and Libraries

ISBN : 978-93-87698-82-6
Price : Rs. 825/-

First Published 2020

Published by:
Ess Ess Publications
4831/24, Ansari Road,
Darya Ganj,
New Delhi-110 002.
INDIA
Phones: 23260807, 41563444
Fax: 41563334
E-mail: info@essessreference.com
www.essessreference.com

Cover Design by *Patch Creative Unit*

Printed and bound in India

Contents

Foreword

Information Science as an academic discipline is often taught in combination with Library Science as Library and Information Science. Library Science as such is a field related to the dissemination of information through libraries making use of the principles of Information science. Information Science is identified as the study of the communication of information in society. It has originated from the needs of the society in addressing the problems in managing information. It is an interdisciplinary science which encompasses Library Science, Information Technology, Computer Science, Cognitive Science, Artificial Intelligence and Communication. In this book important facets of Information Science are delineated in twelve chapters. These include 'Information, Knowledge and Libraries, Information Science as a discipline, Information and its importance, Information and communication process, History of human communication, Properties and behavior of information, Pattern of scientific communication, Barriers of communication process, Bibliometrics, Sociology of information, Economics of information and Information marketing. Each facet is prepared by the author based on intensive study and long term teaching experience in the field of Information science. This knowledge and wisdom acquired by the author have culminated as the outcome of this book. I strongly believe that this book will be a significant contribution in the field of Library and Information science literature. It is hoped that this book will be well received by the students, teachers, Librarians, Information managers and researchers in Library and Information science field in particular and scientific community in general.

6th June 2020 — **Prof. (Dr) G. Devarajan**

Former UGC Emeritus Fellow in Library Science and
Professor & Head , Dept of Library & Information Science,
University of Kerala, Thiruvananthapuram

Preface

The transition from Library Science to Library and Information Science happened during the 1970s. In 1979 we the teachers in the Department of Library and Information Science in the University of Kerala had started working on identifying and listing a course content for the newly proposed Master of Library and Information Science (M.L.I.Sc.) degree programme. Information Science component of the course was only emerging at the international level. A systematic literature search had to be undertaken and accomplished. Thus the four basic areas of concern in Information Science were identified as follows:

(a) Study of information as a basic phenomenon, its nature, properties and behaviour;

(b) Study of Communication Process and the transmission of information;

(c) Study of Information Systems as mechanism by means of which communication process is realized; and

(d) Information and Communication Technology (ICT) as essential tool in the management of information.

From the very beginning of the new M.L.I.Sc. programme, I was directly involved in handling classes for some of the papers. One of my continuous engagement was with the Paper on "*Information, Communication and*

Knowledge" which I taught during my past 50 years of teaching experience. At this fag end of my retired life I thought of writing down what I taught to the generations of students.

This book has been organized into twelve chapters, each dealing with a significant area in the Paper entitled "*Information, Communication and Knowledge*". It is my hope and belief that the book will be meeting an academic need.

I express my sincere gratitude to Mr. Sumit Sethi of Ess Ess Publications, New Delhi for the favour of accepting this book for publishing.

Trivandrum, — **Prof. C. A. Augustine**

Dated: 07-06-2020.

1

Information, Knowledge And Libraries

The nature and scope of Information studies in the special context of Library and Information Science (LIS) studies is worth examining in detail. It is a fact that non-librarians will find it difficult to recognize the claim of librarians for identification with Information Science field. This is because the predominant claimants to this field now are scientists who have in a way confused Information Technology with information science. Although Information Technology is also part of Information Science, it is not the whole of it. Technology is important as it is technology that functions as the carrier of information. Nevertheless, information itself has an identity of its own having been distinct from Information Technology and Communication Technology. However, information can be studied in a wider perspective as a subject by itself. This is what is attempted here throughout this and the subsequent chapters of the book. in this chapter, the discussion is proposed to be concerned with the concepts of information and Knowledge in the context of the Social Environment.

THE SOCIAL ENVIRONMENT

It is a well accepted sociological theory that man is the product of his environment. Auguste Comte (1798-1854), the French philosopher -mathematician who coined the term 'sociology,' pointed out that breaking of social phenomena into their elements rendered them meaningless for study whereas these phenomena could be studied only as wholes. This holistic view or approach means that social relations, ideas and customs form a system in which every part is functionally dependent on every other part for both its operation, and for the observer its meaning. Thus to understand the state of a particular phenomenon it is necessary to place it in its social context.

Hence, Library and Information are also phenomena that need to be studied in their social context. We all know that the old concept of the library has changed corresponding to the changing social contexts. Today, the library is much more than what it was about a hundred years ago. Many new dimensions have been added to it, in purpose, function and use. Correspondingly there has been change in the concept of librarianship. From the old custodian of books, librarian has grown to the position of the Information Specialist who can provide almost all kinds of information help needed by the society he serves. His role has become crucial as the role of information in society has become crucial and as information is still mostly in the human records that he is destined to manage.

Information is being increasingly recognized as an important resource in development. Its crucial role in decision-making at all levels and as a significant factor in socio-economic development have made national governments and international organizations to expedite various measures towards its proper conservation, processing and utilization. It is the importance of information for the success of all types of human activities and endeavors that led to its recognition as a commodity where people and organizations are willing to pay for it. This in turn led to an increasing trade or commercial activity in information - what could be called the "Information Industry".

Increased activities in the production and distribution of information led to an "Information Explosion" through a "document explosion". The selection and utilization of appropriate information has become difficult due mainly to the proliferation of documents. This necessitated specialized expertise in information capturing, information storage and retrieval, information analysis and information dissemination. Thus has emerged a class of information specialists with subject background and methodological training. The new developments in information technology enriched the field of information handling in an unprecedented manner with options and opportunities opened up by micrographics, micro computers, satellite communication, laser technology and a few others. With all these developments the library is placed with new challenges for inducting the new information technology in all appropriate forms in improving the information and document handling processes and functions. Corresponding to the changing information environment modern librarianship needed an intellectual foundation suited to the new information environment. This was what made librarianship embrace Information Science. Search for the new intellectual foundation took librarianship in almost all areas of knowledge, broadly speaking, in humanities for a philosophical foundation, in sciences for a scientific foundation, and in social sciences mainly for a sociological foundation. Thus the new discipline known as" Library and Information Science" was evolved as an aggregate of all knowledge useful and relevant in information and document handling. Library and Information Science is inter-disciplinary in nature and multi-dimensional in its scope for specialization.

All these have been mentioned only to establish two major points, that modern librarianship has evolved in the new social context and that the new social context is the one dominated by new information environment. The new environment is one in which information is the major factor in economics, power and politics. The post-industrial society is an information-based society. Karl Marx wrote in 1884 sketching a simple model of a complex, process of economic change as follows: "*the wind mill gives you a society with the feudal lord; the steam mill a society with the industrial capitalist*". At that time the triad of production factors comprised of "land, labour and capital". Had he been writing a century later he might have noted that the power structure is based not so much on the ownership of land, or of the means of production but on the information capability of the society – the capacity to store, control, communicate and utilize information. As we realize today, the world economy, power and politics are governed by the dichotomy between the 'information-rich' and the 'information-poor' nations.

WORD MEANING OF INFORMATION

Considering the fact that information is basically a social phenomenon and any fruitful study of this phenomenon needs to be in its proper societal setting all that were covered above have significant relevance.

Most dictionaries have attempted to define information as knowledge, intelligence, facts, or data which can be used, transferred or communicated. But a closer study of the concept of information will reveal that it is not equal to knowledge.

The Webster's Third New International Dictionary has given the following meanings for the term information:

1. a an endowing with form.
   b obs: The act of animating or inspiring.
   c obs: TRAINING, DISCIPLINE, INSTRUCTION.
   d the communication or reception of knowledge or intelligence <the function of a public library is ~ > <we enclose a price list for your ~ >.
2. Something received or obtained through informing, as
   a. knowledge communicated by others or obtained from investigation, study or instruction.
   b. knowledge of a particular event or situation: INTELLIGENCE, NEWS, ADVICES, <latest ~ from the battle front> <securing ~ about conditions in the upper atmosphere>, ~ bureau>
   c. facts or figures ready for communication or use as distinguished from those incorporated in a formally originated branch of knowledge: DATA, reliable source of ~ >.
   d. a signal (as one of the digits in dialing a telephone number) purposely impressed upon the input of a communication system or a calculating machine.
3. The act of informing against a person or party.
4. a. a formal accusation of a crime made by a prosecuting officer on information brought to his attention as distinguished from an indictment presented by a grand jury: COMPLAINT.
   b. a pleading by an attorney general or other public officer setting forth a civil case or relief in which some public right of the state is asserted.
   c. the document containing the depositions of the witnesses against one accused of crime.
5. The process by which the form of an object of knowledge is impressed upon the apprehending mind so as to bring about the state of knowing.
6. A logical quantity belonging to a propositions and arguments as well as terms and comprising the sum of the synthetical propositions in which the term, proposition or argument taken enters as subject or predicate, antecedent or consequent - see QUANTITY.

7. A numerical quantity that measures the uncertainty in the outcome of an experiment to be performed <when an event occurs whose probability was *p*, the event is said to communicate an amount of ~ *log (1/p)* – W.F.Brown, b. 1904 >, <the amount of ~ is defined, in the simplest cases, to be measured by the logarithm of the number of available choices – C.E. Shannon & Warren Weaver > ". **Syn** see KNOWLEDGE.

(*Webster's Third New International Dictionary of the English Language.* Unabridged, A Merriam-Webster, Editor in Chief: Philip Babcock Gove, Springfield, Mass, USA.)

Two distinct grammatical uses of the word can be identified: One is "information" as a common noun and the other is as an abstract noun derived out of the verb "to inform". When it is used as a common noun (as with senses numbered as 2 and its sub-divisions) information means something which is communicated from one to another. This is the more common usage of the word. It is in this sense that Jesse H. Shera (1972) has used the word "information" to mean "that which is transmitted by the act or process of communication". A closer look at the use of the word as a common noun will reveal that it can mean either what is transmitted in communication or what is received in communication. These two can be different in a communication process.

THE CONCEPT OF INFORMATION

As Klaus Otten (1947) has rightly put it we talk about information with the belief that we know what information is. But when we try to define 'information' we come across a variety of apparently fitting statements although none is universally valid. The many definitions available reflect only subject and context dependent concepts. According to Debons and Cameron (1973) "*one foremost problem facing the development of a science of information is the uncertainty as to what constitutes information*".

So information is a nebulous concept, difficult to define. What about the word meaning? Meanings found in when the word 'information' is used as an abstract noun, (as indicated by the dictionary meanings numbered as 1 and 3, it will mean the process of communication. V.N. Trostinikov (1926), while writing for the Great *Soviet Encyclopedia,* defined information as "*originally, a message transmitted from certain persons to other persons by verbal, written or any other means (for example, with the help of conventional signals or with the use of technological means), as well as the processes themselves or transmission or reception of the message*". Thus the word "information" stands for not only what is communicated - either transmitted or received, but also the very act or process of communication. Dictionary definition numbered as 4 and its sub divisions are in the legal context.

INFORMATION AS A MEASURE

Dictionary definitions numbered as 6 and 7 are in the particular contexts of Logic and Information Theory respectively, both stressing the quantitative measurement in communication. The foregoing analysis of the dictionary meanings reveals that the concept of information is intrinsically bound with communication process.

From the 1920s communication engineers have been using the term "information" in their scholarly deliberations with some special significance. Hartley who extended the Mathematical Theory of Communication first brought out by Harry Nyquist (1928) used the word 'information' to mean "*the logarithm of the number of symbols available to be chosen by the sender and received by the listener*". Further, in 1948 when Claude E. Shannon brought out his paper on the same theory he confirmed the use of the term in that technical sense. For him "information" was a measure based on the reduction of a given finite number of alternatives caused by the perception and interpretation of a signal. Information thus became a quantitative concept for these writers. This concept gained increased acceptance during later years under its new name "Information Theory" which began to be applied also in some behavioural sciences where quantitative methods had possible applications. However, this meaning of the word sounds very much artificial to the common man. It does not have the human element in communication. Further it does not have any substantive relation with the word "inform" from which the word Information has derived. Communication is a human activity and we are concerned about it only because of that.

INFORMATION IN UNCERTAINTY

According to Manfred Kochen (1983), "information" meant during the 1950s "reduction of uncertainty" while in the 1980s "decision-relevant data". These are true in the sense that information is an important ingredient in decision making. Correct decisions can be taken only on the basis of correct information.

INFORMATION IN COMMUNICATION

Information is a concept basic to communication process while communication in turn is a basic activity of human beings. B.C. Vickery (1987) says that the elemental social process is communication. Man communicates in many ways – by means of sounds, gestures, and through developed packets of intelligible information. These packets take different forms as writing, printing, drawing, photographs, sound recordings, instrument traces (as in the case with ECG) and machine readable recordings (as in the case with computer inputs and outputs). These can be generally called Recorded Information or Documents. Every document is a record of human communication which may be graphic, printed or processed. One peculiar feature of information is that although it can be generated and communicated in non-verbal and unrecorded form, eventually almost all such information will get recorded in some form or the other.

Thus documents play a very significant role in human communication. And documents lead to the production of more documents through their re-production, translation, transliteration, commentary or review, etc. Even if much of the information transmitted orally is not recorded resulting in no permanent record, what is already recorded is of a very vast and formidable quantity. The world of today is addressing itself to the complex problem of putting this available information to use. Therefore 'information' is understood today as almost synonymous with recorded information or documents. It is with this information that the librarians are also concerned.

INFORMATION AND KNOWLEDGE

No discussion on 'information' can be complete and meaningful unless it is duly related to the concept of 'knowledge'. The words 'information' and 'knowledge' are often used loosely to mean one and the same thing. But these are not exactly identical or synonymous terms, although they are found to be closely related. They are even concomitant concepts in the sense that the presence of one will imply very often the presence of the other also. Information is not knowledge. To quote W.L. Saunders(1980) *"...information is not in itself knowledge, any more than knowledge is wisdom. But at least information provides raw material, which in due course can lead to new knowledge, if only via the restructuring of existing knowledge'.* How is that information gets transformed into knowledge? There can be different ways of explaining this. Two important approaches deserve to be pointed out here: One is a biological interpretation while the other is a logical interpretation.

The biological interpretation of knowledge is advanced by people like R.F.A. Hoerule (1952). According to this, knowledge is what we perceive by our senses. But not only human beings do know or perceive. The ability to sense and perceive is a basic quality of life. But perceptions of a developed order will include other faculties like remembering, thinking and reasoning. It is true that plants and animals also perceive objects and situations that they come across. But between the response of plants and animals there is difference and that is the difference of mind. Mind denotes the latest in the three planes of evolution: namely, matter, life and mind. And it is with mind that knowledge emerges. Mind represents a developed state only in the human beings and therefore knowledge occurs only in human beings. This means that knowledge is not just the responses to stimuli. *"To know is, therefore, to perceive and to think truly; to perceive and think things as they are. But in actual practice perceiving and thinking by different persons may succeed or fail - both in varying degrees – to realize the truth"* (Hoerule 1952). Knowledge should have the quality of truth. Mistakes and errors are not knowledge. Knowing is the mind's activity and 'knowledge' is what is so known.

The logical interpretation of knowledge is given by people like John Dewey (1938). In the scientific method of enquiry the word 'knowledge' represents that which emerges as the outcome of competent enquiry. But enquiry itself is a continuing process in any field. We cannot say that anything is final or settled as the outcome of our enquiry. Dewey wrote: *"The settlement of a particular situation by a particular enquiry is no guarantee that settled conclusions will always remain settled ... It is the convergent and cumulative effect of continued enquiry that defines knowledge in its general meaning"*. Knowledge once settled will be available as resource for further enquiry.

Both the above interpretations throw light on one and the same thing. Information is that which is perceived and subjected to a mental process. As the mental abilities in perceiving and processing information will be different in different individuals knowledge is personal and subjective by nature. The total of all such personal knowledge is the knowledge of the mankind.

THE GROWTH PROCESS OF KNOWLEDGE

Information as explained earlier is the raw data for knowledge. Information is converted into knowledge by a process of mind. The eminent biologist Paul Weiss (1964) has brought out an analogy between growth process in knowledge and in organisms. According to him, "*fundamentally, our knowledge grows the way a living body does*". He states, "*scientific knowledge grows like an organic tree, not as a compilation of collector's items. Facts, observations, discordances, as items are but the nutrients on which the tree of knowledge feeds, and not until they have been thoroughly absorbed and assimilated, have they truly enlarged the body of knowledge*" . To expound this thesis Weiss has selected the model of a higher animal and the main steps of its growth process are shown diagrammatically side by side with the growth process of knowledge.

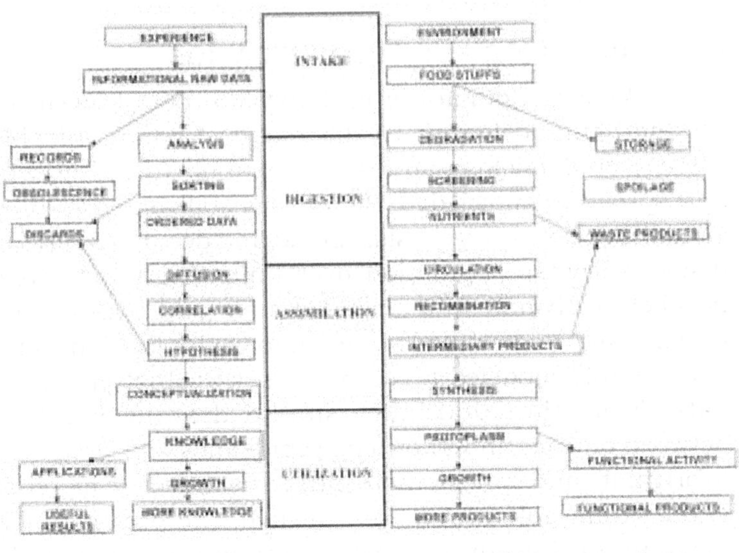

(*Source* : Paul Weiss: Knowledge – a growth Process (1964))

According to Goffman and Newill (1970) Communication of ideas by recorded discourse is assumed to be governed by processes formally equivalent to communication of disease by micro-organisms and of signals by machines. They have introduced the theory of intellectual epidemics as a model of scientific communication. According to this model the diffusion of ideas in a population of scientists could be compared to the spreading of an influenza virus in a population of people, causing an epidemic.

"information" and " knowledge " are not synonymous terms. Information may lead to knowledge, It is the precursor of knowledge. The growth process in knowledge is comparable to the growth process in higher animals. As the growth of the latter is caused by the intake of food stuffs, from the environment through a process of degradation, screening, recombination, and synthesis, information is raw data collected from experience which is analyzed, sorted, correlated, and conceptualized to become finally the part of existing knowledge.

EPIDEMIC THEORY OF COMMUNICATION

"William Goffman is probably the best known for his mathematical work in the realm of communicable disease epidemiology and its application to the growth and spread of knowledge. He and his colleagues studied similarities between genesis, spread and decline of various diseases across population over time. They then drew parallels with how human individuals and populations become "infected" with ideas and knowledge fashions, and successfully modeled these processes against empirical data. From the 1960s they started drawing parallels between disease and knowledge epidemics. For a disease to originate and spread, there must exist infective material and a vulnerable population. In turn, the population is made up of "infectives" (hosts to the infective material), "susceptible" (those who can be infected), and "removals" (those who are susceptible or infected but leave the population because of immunity, hospitalization, or death). Exposed individuals are either immune to the disease or can become infected through contact with a disease host or vector. The time required for an infective to develop the disease after contact with infectious material is known as "latency" or incubation period. An epidemic may be said to occur when a disease outbreak involved an abnormally high number of individuals. Goffman and Neville extended the above epidemic concepts by discussing various knowledge epidemics, such as the spread of major religious ideas and such scientific concepts as those of Newton, Darwin an Freud. But they noted that while most idea epidemics might be regarded as desirable, disease epidemics are generally not desired. Vulnerable members of a scientific or lay population could, for example, be infected with a concept published in a book or journal (a vector), while other members, being immune, might reject that concept. Or, immune individuals might transmit the concept without being infected (the "Typhoid Mary" phenomenon). Once an abnormally large number of population members become infected with the concept, a knowledge epidemic can be said to occur" (Glynn Harmon,2008).

DATA AND INFORMATION

According to Manfred Kochen (1964) "*information is decision-relevant data*". In the words of Whittemore and Yovits (1972) "*Information is data of value to decision making*". Data may be considered signs, usually recorded observations, that are not currently affecting behaviour. However, data becomes information if behavior becomes affected. For example, the massive data contained in a computer data base are only signs that are not affecting behaviour. Until the data are actually viewed, and are properly organized for a person who reacts to them, they are not information. Information is the net value obtained from the process of matching the elements of a present problem with appropriate elements of data

THE DIKW PYRAMID

The relationship between data, information and knowledge is better illustrated through a diagram showing the DIKW Pyramid as shown below:

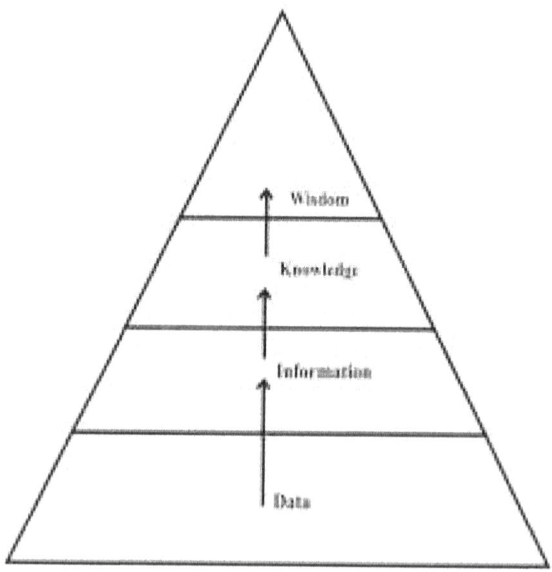

Fig. 1.2. The DIKW Pyramid (Danny P. Wallace, 2007)

The pyramid represents purported structural and/ or functional relationships between data, information, knowledge and wisdom. In the words of Jennifer Rowley (2007) "*Typically information is defined in terms of data and information, in terms of information and knowledge, and in terms of knowledge and wisdom*". Danny P. Wallace (2007), a professor of Library and Information Science, explained that the origin of the DIKW Pyramid is uncertain, although it has been part of the language of information science for many years It is said that the Pyramid originated from the play, *The Rock* by T. S. Eliot in 1934. It contained the following lines:

"Where is the life we have lost in living?,

Where is the wisdom we have lost in knowledge?

Where is the knowledge we have lost in Information?"

Since then, the pyramid was modified by many a writers. (*en.m. wilikpedia.org)*.

INFORMATION CONCEPT FOR INFORMATION SCIENCE

The discussion so far has been to bring out two major notions about information:

1. Information is that which is transmitted or received in a communication process including all forms of recorded information, and
2. Information is not in itself knowledge but it may lead to new knowledge or restructuring of existing knowledge.

These two notions are of direct relevance and concern to Information Science. Information Science, in this context, has to be understood as the discipline dealing with the scientific study of communication of information in society (Vickery & Vickery (1987). And in the context of Library and Information Science it is the study of communication of recorded information.

REFERENCES

COMTE, Auguste, (1865), *A General View of Positvism (Discours sur l'ensemble du positivism, 1848*), tr. by J.H.Bridges, Trubner & co.

Debons, A. and Cameron, J. *Eds.* "Editorial Summary" *in Perspectives of Information Science; the proceedings of the second NATO Advanced Study Institutes, Wales , 1973.*

DEWEY, John. *Logic, the theory of enquiry.* New York, Henry Holt &Co, '1938.

DIKW Pyramid *en.m.wikipedia.org,*dated 25-04-2020.

DURKHEIM, Emile (1919) *The Rules of Sociological Method and Selected Texts on Sociology and its Method* ed. by Steven Lukes, and tr. by W. D. Halls, New York, The Free Press (1895), Paris.

HOERULE, R F A (1952), *Studies in philosophy* ed by Daniel S. Robinson, London, A.G. Allen &Thomas, 1952.

ELIOT, T.S.(1934), *Choruses from the Rock*, Poetry Nook, 1934.

GOFFMAN, W. and NEVILLE, V.A. (1964), "Communication and Epidemic Processes" *in Proceedings of the Royal Society of London, Series A: Mathematical and Physical Sciences*, Vol.298 No.1454 (May 2, 1967), Pp.316-334.

GOFFMAN, W. and NEVILLE, V.A. (1964) "A General Theory of Communication", ("Epidemic Theory of Communication; Epidemic model of the spread of scientific ideas as manifested by publication") *in* SARACEVIC, Tefko (1970), *Introduction to information Science*, Pp 726- , R.R. Bowker & Co, 1970.

HARMON, Glynn (2008) "Remembering William Goffman: Mathematical Information Science Pioneer" *in Information Processing and Management, Vol* XXX (2008) (*www.sciencedirect.com*).

KOCHEN, MANFRED (1964), *The Growth of Knowledge*, N.Y. John Wiley, 1964.

KOCHEN, Manfred (1983), "Information and Society" *ARIST* 18 (1983) pp.277-304.

MARX. Karl (1844), *Economic and Philosophic Manuscripts of 1844*, Moscow, Progress Publications, 1959.

NYQUIST, Harry (1928) "Certain Topics In Telegraph Transmission Theory", *Trans. AAIEE*, Vol 47, pp 617-644, April 1928.

OTTEN, Klaus W. (1974), "Basis For A Science of Information" *in* Debons, A. *Ed. Information Science; Search for Identity*, New York, Marcel Dekker, 1974 pp.91-100.

ROWLEY, Jennifer (2007) "The Wisdom hierarchy representations of the DIKW Hierarchy" *in Journal of Information and Communication Science*, 33(2):163-180.

SATYANARAYANA, N. R. (1966): *Information Technology and Its Facets*, New Delhi, Manal.

SATYANARAYANA, N.R and SATYANARAYANA, R. (1996) : Problems of Information Science, New Age International,1996.

SAUNDERS, W.L. (1980), "Information the unscarce resources" *in The Proceedings of the Joint Conference of ASLIB, the Institute of Information Scientists and Library Association held in September 1980,* pages 1-12.

SHANNON, Claude E. (1948),"A Mathematical Theory of Communication" *The Bell System Technical; Journal,* 27(3):379-423, 1948.; Shannon, Claude E. and Weaver, Warren, *The Mathematical Theory of Communication,* Chicago, University of Illinois Press, 1948.

SHERA, Jesse H., *Foundations of Education for Librarianship,* N.Y. Wiley, Becker and Hayes, 1972 pp.164.

SIMON, Andrews (2000): "Information Science: Historical and Social Aspects, A World Outlook" *Journal of Documentation,* 56:p.12-14.

TROSTINIKOV, V.N. (1926), "Information Science" *in Great Soviet Encyclopedia* Volume 10, PP. 274.

VICKERY, B.C. and VICKERY, Alina (1987), *Information Science in theory and practice,* London, Butterworth, 1987.

WALLACE , Danny P. (2007) *Knowledge Management: Historical and Cross-Disciplinary Themes,* Libraries Unlimited, Pp.1-14.

Webster's Third New International Dictionary of the English Language. Unabridged, A Merriam-Webster, Editor in Chief: Philip Babcock Gove, Springfield, Mass, USA.S

WEISS, Paul (1964), "Knowledge - A Growth Process" *in* Kochen, Manfred, *ed, The growth of knowledge,* N.Y., John Wiley, 1964 pp. 209-215.

WHITTEMORE, B.J. and YOVITS, M.C. (1972), *A Generalized Conceptual Development for the Analysis and Flow of Information,* Ohio State University, Columbus Computer Science Research Centre, 35 P.

2

Information Science As A Discipline

We do not know for certain when where the term 'information science' was first used. There is an information that the first known usage of the term information science was in 1955 (*www.merriam-webster.co.* On the contrary, in 1959, the Moore School of Electronic Engineering, University of Pennsylvania, US, was reported to have first used the term Information Science, but it only referred to a description of a computer programme and not a theory of information. (*en.m.wikipedia.org*). There is also a counter claim the term 'Information Science' was first used by J. Farradane in 1962. However, in the year 1968 there were two significant events worth reporting in this connection. At first, the American Documentation Institute changed its name to Association for Information Science and Technology and its official journal *American Documentation* changed its name to *Journal of the Association for Information Science and Technology* in the year 1968. Secondly, the FID adopted the word 'Information' to its name into

"International Federation for Information and Documentation" in 1988. Two international events occurred before this time. The first was the First NATO Advanced Study Institute on Information Science was held in USA in 1972. The proceedings of this conference addressed two issues: (a) developing a 'true science of information'; and (b) developing a practical domain of information systems design, implementation, management and use. The Second such Advanced Study Institute was held on "Perfection of Information Science" in UK in 1973. The four areas of concern then were: (a)the nature of information; (b) information technology and its ability to meet human needs; (c) the impact of information technology on man; and (d) professional aspects. In 1977 a chapter entitled "History and Foundations of Information Science" appeared in the *Annual Review of Information Science and Technology,* under the authorship of Michael K During the 1970s and 1980s the trend was that library schools all over the world began modifying their names and insignia of degrees awarded in favour of information science. Accordingly, the University of Kerala, along with most of the universities in India changed the names of the courses and the degrees awarded as B.L.I.Sc and M.L.I.Sc. from the old B.Lib.Sc. and M.Lib.Sc. respectively. Naturally, Library Science was changing towards Library & Information Science.

The question that arises here in this context is whether Library Science and Information Science are two separate subjects or one is part of the other. Generally speaking, it can be just a shift in emphasis from books and documents to 'information' as the major concern of library education. But, is that all?

Not only librarians but also others are interested and involved in study of information. Who else are they? They are those who were involved in communication of information. In order to know who are they one has to view the communication process in detail. Communication process is a sequence of events involved in taking a message from the source and transmitting it to the destination. There are three basic elements in this process: (i) Source (ii) Message, and (iii) Destination. Two more elements are there that are optional: (iv) Medium and (v) Meaning.

Source may be an *individual* speaking, writing, drawing or gesturing; or an *organization*, like newspaper publishing house, television studio, etc, or a *machine*, like a radar /automatic control system.

Message is the information, news, feelings, expressions, desires, commands, instructions, etc.

Medium can be verbal or non-verbal. (Verbal like oral, written, or recorded otherwise) or Non-verbal like signs, symbols).

COMMUNICATION PROCESS

Communication Model

Source → Encoder → Medium → Message → Decoder → Medium → Destination

Source → Encoder → Medium → Channel → Message → Decoder → Destination → Noise →

Communication process involves three sets of problems, i.e.

(a) Physical / Technical problems;

(b) Semantic / Linguistic problems, and

(c) Behavioural / Human problems.

Those concerned with physical/ technical problems are the engineers, and technological scientists in communication engineering. From the side of the semantic problems there are the linguists, programmers, etc. From behavioural/ human side are the psychologists, and mass communication experts. Thus experts from all these different areas are engaged in Information studies. Information is intrinsically bound with human communication. Communication is basic to human existence and development. Therefore, subject of information is of social significance and relevance. Consequent to the increasing importance of information and communication process there is increased significance and relevance of Information Science.

RELEVANCE OF INFORMATION SCIENCE FOR LIBRARY MANAGERS

Relevance of Information Science for library managers is born out of the social significance of the Library. The library has a definite role in human communication of knowledge, ideas and information. Oral communication has the serious limitation because it is time bound and space bound. One can communicate with another who is currently present within an audible distance. It was mainly to overcome the above limitation, that the recorded communication was evolved. Almost simultaneously, the library became a resting place for the recorded message. It enables interpersonal, inter-cultural and inter-generation communication. The library is so to say the social memory. The successive stages through which this social memory evolved are the archives, manuscript libraries, libraries of printed books, and electronic libraries. Commensurate with this evolution the discipline concerning the management of libraries also evolving like the following: For the *Archives* custodianship and inventory control were necessary. For the *Manuscript Library,* functions like copying, curing, editing, listing and describing the documents were warranted. In the case of the *Library of Printed Books,* activities like classification, cataloguing, developing issue methods, collection development, book selection, etc. were in the beginning and later Personal Assistance and Reference Service, and still later Documentation including indexing, abstracting and reprography. In the case of the Modern Library concentrated activities aimed at information storage and retrieval, introduction of information technology and computerization, information analysis, information repackaging, information systems management, etc were additionally required to be undertaken. Thus, library management at present is a fast evolving profession involving different areas of specialization.

GENESIS OF INFORMATION SCIENCE

The term "Information Science" had its genesis outside library profession. It first appeared in the guise of information scientist. Particularly in industry, during the recent decades some qualified scientists moved out of research, development or production into a new occupational role of providing active information services to their colleagues. They regarded themselves as "information scientists" rather than "research scientists". As this kind of work expanded and became formalized the need was seen to provide training for those who would enter the occupation. In time, the content of this training came to be called "information science" (Vickery, B.C. 1987). Information Science is born out of the importance of information for individual and society. The demand for information was responded by the emergence of information industry producing and marketing all types of information. This situation required development of information systems for collecting, organizing, and accessing information. This in turn necessitated specialized personnel to manage the information systems. These information specialists contributed to the emergence of the new "information profession" with subject background, competence and methodology in the selection, analysis and interpretation of information. They came to be designated differently, as special librarian, documentation officer, documentalist, information officer, information manager or information scientist. What followed was the essential conceptualization and formation of an academic discipline comprehending systematized knowledge that are found useful or applicable in the work of the information specialists, namely 'Information Science'.

DEFINITION OF INFORMATION SCIENCE

As pointed out earlier, Information Science as a discipline had its origin and development outside the library profession. It has evolved as an inter-disciplinary science from such fields as Mathematics, Logic, Linguistics, Psychology, Computer Technology, Operation Research, Graphic Arts, Communication, Management, and other fields including Library Science. According to B.C. Vickery *(1987) " Information Science is the study of communication of information in society". The Webster's New Collegiate Dictionary (1977)* defined Information Science as *"the collection, classification, storage, retrieval and dissemination of recoded knowledge treated as both a pure and applied science".* According to *Encyclopaedia Britannica (2001) "Information Science is the discipline that deals with the processes of storing and transferring information. It attempts to bring together concepts and methods from various disciplines such as library science, computer science and engineering, linguistics, psychology and other technologies in order to develop techniques ad devices to aid in the handling – that is in the collection, organization, storage, retrieval, interpretation, and use – of information"* According to the same source *"Information Science is the acquisition, recording, organization, retrieval, display, and dissemination of information. In recent years, the term has often been applied to computer based operations specifically".*

Harold Borko (1968) defined Information Science as *"a body of knowledge relating to the origination, collection, organization, storage, retrieval, interpretation, transmission, transformation and utilization of information".* To quote Borko *(1968) further at length, "Information science is that discipline that investigates the properties and behaviour of information, the forces governing the flow of information, and the means of processing information for optimum accessibility and usability. It is concerned with that body of knowledge relating to the origination collection organization, storage, retrieval, interpretation, transmission, transformation, and utilization of information. This includes the investigation of information representations in both natural and artificial systems, the use of codes for efficient message transmission, and the study of information processing devices and techniques such as computers and their programming systems. It is an interdisciplinary science derived from and related to such field as mathematics, logic, linguistics, psychology, operations research, the graphic arts, communications, management, and other similar fields. It has both a pure science component, which inquires into the subject without regard to its application, and an applied science component, which develops, services and products" (Borko, 1968 p.3)*

Tefko Saracevic in the *Introduction to Information science* wrote: "*Information Science aims at being a unified scientific approach to the study of various phenomena connected with the notion of information. These phenomena can be found in biological processes as well as in human existence, and the machines created by human beings. Thus the subject has evolved as a synthesis of methods drawn from the traditional disciplines for the purpose of studying the multi-varied aspects of information flow within a population of objects, be they human beings, micro organisms or machines. Information Science, therefore, is essentially concerned with the principles underlying communication processes and their associated information systems*".

A former Executive Director of the American Society for Information Science defined Information Science for a report as follows: "*Information Science is the study of how information is transferred from the point of generation to the point of use and all the intermediate steps of collecting, organizing, interpreting, storing, retrieving, disseminating and transferring of information. As a discipline information science stresses the application of modern technologies to the harnessing of information".*

According to John Gray and Brian Perry (1975*): "Information Science is that area of knowledge which deals with the information –its various problems, properties and behaviour; the flow of information - the process of information transfer, the media, the channels, their impediments , etc; the design of information systems and their evaluation - including traditional systems of publication of records, libraries, information storage and retrieval systems and systems based on manual methods and mechanical methods including the use of electronic computers"*

CONTENT OR SCOPE OF INFORMATION SCIENCE

As Information Science is interdisciplinary in nature, It has borrowed heavily from various traditional disciplines like: Philosophy, Psychology, Linguistics, Physics, Engineering, Chemistry, Communication Studies, Communication Engineering, Computer Technology, According to Anthony Debons, etc., "Information Science historically has, many primary roots. One being epistemology, or the study of knowledge. In the modern sense, information scientists are primarily concerned with two basic fundamentals: the need "to count and account and to record and communicate". Many disciplines contributed to the science of information. The 4 basic disciplines that are most important to the study of information are: Philosophy (rules of logic, inquiry systems, foundations of social sciences), Mathematics (Statistics, quantification and measure), Linguistics (representing, and communicating), and Behavioural Sciences (all branches of psychology and sociology). The related fields are: informatics (origin in 1960s; study of automation and automated technologies in document retrieval); Information Engineering (design of information systems); Knowledge Engineering (expert systems and artificial intelligence), and Cybernetics (scientific control).

The 1972 NATO Advanced Study Institute in Information Science reported that "there is a great need to create, develop; and strengthen a theoretical foundation for information science. This theoretical foundation was seen to focus on solid, consistent, theoretical explication of the notion of information. Thus the task at hand was to study the fundamental principles underlying the structure and use of information". The Institute's proceedings were addressed to two issues: (a) developing a "true" science of information; (b) developing a practical domain of information system design, implementation, management and use. (Debons and Cameron, 1972). "Thus the task of studying the nature of information is to facilitate information science's becoming a *science* and to facilitate information science's contributing to society in terms of better designed information systems" (Rathswohl,1972). In the 1973 NATO –ASI Conference held on 13-24 August 1973 in Wales, the four areas of concern were listed as: (1) The nature of information, (2) Information technology and activity to meet human needs, (3) the impact of information technology on man, and (4)professional aspects.

SCOPE OF INFORMATION SCIENCE FOR LIBRARIANS

B.C. Vickery in 1987 summarized the scope of Information Science which include among others:

- The behaviour of people as generators, sources, recipients, and users of information, all of whom are partners in information transfer process;
- The quantitative study of messages: its size, growth rate, distribution, patterns of production and use;
- The semantic organization of messages and of channels that facilitates their identification by sources and recipients;

- Problems particularly associated with the functions of information storage, analysis and retrievals;
- The overall organization of information systems and their performance in transfer;
- The social context of information transfer, in particular its economics and politics. (VICKERY, B.C. (1987).

Ranganathan's Five Laws of Library Science examined in the light of the canvass of information science, give the widest implications of information as it is evolving today which also fits in with the contours of Vickery. Restated with emphasis on information, the five laws are:

Information is for use

Every User his / her information

Every Information its user

Save the time of the user

Information system is a growing organism.

According to the Curriculum Committee of the Special Interest Group of the American Society for Information Science (1974) the 9 subjects which have a bearing on studies in Information Science are:

1. Psychology/Behavioural Sciences,
2. Language / Linguistics,
3. Management Studies,
4. Statistics,
5. Library Science,
6. System Analysis,
7. Mathematics,
8. Information /Communication Theory, and
9. Computer Science /Automation.

American Universities in the 1980s suggested 7 courses in Information Science:

1. Introduction to Information Science

2. System Theory & Application
3. Mathematical Methods in Information Science
4. Computer Organizing and Programming Systems
5. Abstracting/Indexing/Cataloguing
6. Information & Communication Theory
7. Research Methods

FOUR BROAD AREAS IN INFORMATION SCIENCE

A cursory view of the above discussions on the curriculum content as are given by different authorities makes it too difficult to delineate the true components of Information Science as a new discipline. We in the Department of Library and Information Science, University of Kerala, were addressing ourselves to the task of identifying the important sectors in the curriculum for which we made a literature survey as early as in 1980 which helped us to list the important possible sectors in the course curriculum (Pushpa Raghaviah and C.A. Augustine, 1980).

The four major broad areas of study in the Information Science, over and above the traditional subjects of Library Science discipline, are:

1. Information as a phenomenon –its nature, properties and behavior.
2. Communication Process – methods, media, and channels involved and behavioural, representational and technical problems inherent in information transfer.
3. Information Systems – their design and evaluation.
4. Information and Communication Technology – as tools in communication and information transfer.

As belonging to these 4 major areas, the following 17 sectors could be identified and listed as a result of the above mentioned study:

1. Information Science – definition and scope;
2. Information and its uses;
3. Information and Communication Process;
4. Properties and Behaviour of Information;
5. User Needs and Behaviour;
6. Information Systems in Communication Process;
7. Bibliographic Control and Organization;
8. Information Storage and Retrieval;
9. Indexing Techniques;
10. Indexing Languages;
11. Abstracting;
12. Information Services;
13. Reprography;
14. Library Automation;
15. Computer Methods;
16. Computerized Information Systems; and
17. System Analysis and Design.

In course of time there were subsequent changes in the syllabus or course content but they were only so as to say minor, changes that became necessary in view of the changing trends in library and information science education.

REFERENCES

AMERICAN SOCIETY FOR INFORMATION SCIENCE, ASIS-EIS Curriculum Committee (1974), *Continuing Library and Information Science Education: Final Report* by Elizabeth W. Stone, and Ruth J. Patrick (1974).

BORKO, H. "Information Science: What is it?", *American Documentation*, 1968, 19(1):3-5.

DEBONS, Anthony (1988), *Information Science; an integrated view*, G.K. Hall & Co. Boston.

DEBONS, A. and CAMERON, W.J.(1972), *Perspectives in Information Science; proceedings of the 1972 NATO Advanced Study*

Institute In Information Science, University of Pittsburgh, USA.

Encyclopaedia Britannica, 2001.

FARRADANE, J. and MALCOM, G.(1962), "Education in Information Work: the syllabus and present curriculum of the Institute of Information Science, Ltd.", *Journal of Chemical Documentation*, Vol.2 (1962): pp.74-76.

GRAY, John and PERRY, Brian,(1975) *Scientific Information*, London, O.U.P. *https://en.m.wikipedia.org.*

Journal of American Society for Information Science (JASIS) (1974) 25:77-85.

MICHAEL, K. "History of Foundations of Information Science" *in Annual Review of Information Science and Technology* Vol. 12 (1977): 249-75.

RAGHAVIAH, Pushpa and AUGUSTINE , C. A. (1980), *Identification of the Core Literature in Information Science for the Master of Library & Information Science Programme and An Evaluation of the Kerala University Library Book Collection in the Area;* Dissertation submitted to the University of Kerala in partial fulfillment of the requirements of the Degree of Master of Library and Information Science, Department of Library & Information science, University of Kerala, Trivandrum, 1980.

RATHSWOHL, Eugene J.(1972) "N*ature of information"*, in Debons, H. and Cameron, W.J. *Perspectives in Information Science,* Univ. of Pittsburgh, 1972,P. 21.

SARACEVIC, Tefko (1970), *Introduction to Information Science*, R.R. Bowker & Co. P.726.

VICKERY, Alan and VICKERY, B.C. *(1987) Information Science in theory and practice, Butterworths, P.387.*

www.merriam-webster.co retrieved on 25-09-2017.

3

Information and Its Importance

The emergence of Information Science has been consequent to the increasing importance of information. Therefore, it is relevant to understand what is information, the different types of information, and the major uses of information.

DEFINING INFORMATION

The term 'information' is rather difficult to define. It has been given various shades of meanings in a variety of contexts. Information is defined by dictionaries as knowledge, intelligence, facts or data which can be used, transferred or communicated. Some of the larger dictionaries like the Webster's Third New International Dictionary give several senses of meanings. In one sense information means something which is communicated from one to another. This is the more common sense meaning of the term. This is also the sense in which librarians and others engaged in the field of information storage and retrieval often use the term 'information'. To quote Jesse H. Shera information *"is that which is transmitted by the act or process of communication; it may be a message, a signal, a stimulus"*, V.N. Troshinikov in the *Great Soviet Encyclopaedia* (1983) has defined information as *"originally, a message transmitted from certain persons to other persons by verbal, written or any other means (for example, with the help of conventional signals or with the use of technological means), as well as the processes themselves or transmission or reception of the message).*

Thus information is that which is communicated, either transmitted or received. Man communicates in many ways- Not only by means of sounds and gestures, but also through durable, more or less permanent, packets of intelligible information, in such forms as writing, printing, drawing, photograph, sound recordings, instrument traces (as in ECG). We can call them generally, 'Recorded Communication'. As librarians and information specialists, we are mainly concerned with these packets of information. These packets or records are accumulating by millions each year, which can be collectively described as "Records". These information are important but for that they would not have been produced at all, kept at all, and used at all.

INFORMATION AND ITS USES

Information has many uses. Wherever communication is important there are information is in use. The multi-various use of information can be generally listed as hereunder:

- Information in education;
- Information in research and development;
- Information in business and industry;
- Information in Government – judiciary, legislature and executive;
- Information in international understanding;

- Information in defense, war, diplomacy and peace;
- Information in the economic, political and social life of the individual;
- Information in the development of culture;
- Etc., etc.

Thus information is almost an universal, all pervasive phenomenon.

INFORMATION IN DECISION-MAKING

One basic area of information use is in decision making. Information is an important ingredient in decision making. Information input involves reduction of uncertainty. That is what the decision maker expects from an information system. The degree of uncertainty of the decision maker can vary, and so the amount of information needed or taken from the system will also vary. Information used is thus of a relative quantity and can be quantified in terms of its effects on the state of the decision maker at a particular amount of time. Too much information can also increase uncertainty.

PLACE OF SCIENTIFIC INFORMATION

Information is therefore an essential resource both for the individual and for the society, comparable to other resources, like resources of nature – land, minerals and water; resources of capital, labour, intellectual man power and human skills. This crucial importance of information or its indispensability, demands that information has to be adequately produced, distributed and consumed, like any other essential commodity.

If information generally is an indispensable resource for the society, scientific information is a more vital resource. This is because today science and society are so intertwined as to make the present society of ours a scientific and technological society.

What is scientific information? It is the result of

scientific research. Research as we understand is of two types: (a) Basic and Fundamental research, (b) Applied or Practical research. Results of research at both levels are significant information for the society. The results of Basic Research are of direct interest mainly to other research workers – either at the Basic Research level or at the Applied Research level. But they are not of any direct application or significance to the common man, other than for satisfying the curiosity of general knowledge, whereas, the results of Applied Research and Development concern virtually all types of information users.

What then is Technical Information? Scientific information extracted from its sources and put together in different packages become known as Technical Information. The need for such scientific or technical information in the modern society is increasingly evident. They are needed for decision making at all levels, for conduct of research, for development of industries, for support of education, for development of skills, and for multifarious application in practical life.

Scientific information, therefore, needs to be communicated or transferred in suitable forms to several kinds of users: to fellow scientists, to decision makers, and to various practitioners. But, this process of scientific information transfer creates major problems of presentation and handling with changes in emphasis, grouping, and level of treatment to suit different requirements. Information can take any form and can be combined in different packages. It can be either personal communication - oral or written, or mass communication – like a public lecture, printed publication in conventional form, or in micrographic form, or magnetic record. In treatment of content it can range from a full description of research findings to compilation of bibliographies of all kinds, popular digests, and reviews. Any how, the problem of scientific information has to be tackled in the best way possible, organizing the available resources in the best way to satisfy the broad range of needs. If the problem of scientific information is not solved it will lead to unbearable waste of money, time and energy. According to 1969 statistics 9% of the research expenditure may be wasted, either (1) because research is unintentionally duplicated, or (2) because it could have been planned more soundly, or (3) because it could have been executed more efficiently — in any case due only to lack of proper information.

CONSEQUENCES OF THE REALIZATION

There are several consequences of realizing the importance of information. Some of these are discussed hereunder: (Grey & Perry,1975).

1. Information Industry

Encyclopaedia of Communication and Information (2002) has defined information industry: "*information industry comprises a group of enterprises and organizations whose purpose is to produce, process information and to develop the infrastructure and delivery mechanisms to disburse information*". According to the American Information Industry Association (1988), information is a combination of production activities that produce and provide information products and services by utilizing new technologies and innovative information processing methods. The four components of information industry are the authors, the publishers, the distributors and the users.

In the beginning information industry was only an area under occupation of scientific societies and organizations. Later, governments entered the field in a large scale. And still later, commercial agencies began to occupy the field.

Corresponding to the development of this information industry there has been increasing recognition of the importance of information and its belter use.

2. Information Systems

An information system is an organized procedure for collecting, processing, storing, and retrieving information to satisfy a variety of user needs. Firstly, the increasing recognition of the importance of information made it necessary to have some deliberate arrangements made for the storage and retrieval of information by collecting, organizing, and making accessible the records of all the relevant information. These are the Information Systems. For example are the Libraries, Documentation Centres, Information Centres, Information Analysis Centres, Referral Centres, Information Storage & Retrieval Systems, Databases/Data banks, etc. These are all among the outcome of the above realization.

Secondly, in all kinds of organizations, may be industrial companies, government establishments, business firms, research and development institutes, increasing attention began to be paid to the design and development of information systems to meet their complex information needs. For example are the Integrated Management Information Systems devised to provide managers at all levels with up-to-date information needed for important decisions.

Thirdly, in Governments, whether at Central, State or Local level, the range of activities have become so wide that their information needs have to be handled in separate information systems like one for legislative system, one for criminal and police records, another for planning, one for medical records, one for educational statistics and so on.

Finally, although these information systems are designed and put into operation by different organizations and establishments for different purposes, the broad aim of each such system remained the same, i.e. to collect all information needed for sound and timely decisions and to promote its effective use.

3. Information Networks

A network is a physically separate computers with telecommunication links through which they can exchange information and share resources. More economic utilization of the available resources - men, materials, and money – in meeting the increasing information needs led to establishment of integrated information systems and networking arrangements with a view to sharing the resources on a mutual benefit basis.

4. Information Specialists

Sensible use of information depends to a large extent on human selection and analysis and interpretation. This led to the emergence of a profession having members who have the necessary subject qualification, competence and methodology known as Information Specialists. They may be either working as Special Librarians, Documentation Officers, Documentalists, Information Officers, or Information Scientists, who are known by a myriad of names.

5. Information Technology

The realization of the importance of information also led to the induction of modern technology for the storage, retrieval and dissemination of information. This was originally in two main areas: Micrographics and Computerized Information Storage and Retrieval. The dictionary definition of 'micrographics' is the production of text or graphic images in a photographically reduced form that requires the use of a machine to be viewed. According to the *ALA Glossary*, the application of computers and other technologies to the acquisition, organization, storage, retrieval and dissemination of information came to be addressed generally as Information Technology. Later, the unique combination of developments in the processing, storage, and dissemination of oral, pictorial, textual, animated and numerical information, computer technology and telecommunication technology led to the emergence and development of a new discipline called 'Information and Communication Technology'. The components of lICT can be broadly grouped under (1) Computer Technology, (2) Telecommunication Technology, and (3) Storage Technology.

6. Information Science

The emergence of the profession of Information Specialists was followed by attempts at conceptualization and formation of an academic discipline, comprehending systematized knowledge found useful or applicable in the work of the information specialists. Thus was born a new discipline called 'Information Science'.

Information Science is so inter-disciplinary in nature that it has borrowed heavily from various traditional disciplines like Philosophy, Psychology, Linguistics, Physics, Engineering, Chemistry, Communication Studies, Computer Technology, etc.

In general, Information Science is that area of knowledge which deals with

(i) the information - its various problems, properties and behaviour;

(ii) the flow of information - the process of information transfer, the media, the channels, their impediments, etc; and

(iii) the design of information systems and their evaluation – including traditional systems of publication of records, libraries, information storage and retrieval systems, and systems based on manual methods and mechanical methods including the use of electronic computer.

REFERENCES

AMERICAN INFORMATION INDUSTRY ASSOCIATION (1988)," Research and development", by D. Worlock *ASLIB Proceedings* Vol.40 (10) October,1988

ENCYCLOPAEDIA OF COMUNICATION AND INFORMATION (2002), BY Jorge Reina Schement, New York, Macmillan Reference, USA.

GREY, John and PERRY, Brian (1975) *Scientific Information* , London, O.U.P.

SHERA, Jesse H. (1972) *Foundation of Education for Librarianship,* New York, Becker &Hayes.

TROSHINIKOV, V.N. (1983) "Information Science" *in Great Soviet Encyclopaedia, A translation of the third Edition,* Macmillan Publishers.

4

Information and Communication Process

Information is a concept basic to communication process, while communication is a basic activity of human beings. According to B.C. Vickery (1987), communication is the elemental social process. Man communicates in many ways; by means of sounds, gestures, and through different packets of intelligible information. These packets may take different forms, as writing, printing, drawing, photographs, sound recordings, instrumental traces (as in the case of an ECG) and machine readable recordings (as in the case with computer inputs and outputs). All these can be generally called "Recorded Information" or "Documents". Every document is a record of human communication which may be either graphic, printed or processed. One peculiar feature of information is that, although, it can be generated and communicated in non-verbal and recorded form, eventually almost all such information will get recorded in some form or the other. Thus documents play a very significant role in human communication. And documents lead to the production of more documents through their reproduction, translation, transliteration, reformatting, extraction, concordance, indexing, summarization, commentary, review, etc. Even if much of the information transmitted orally is not recorded and results in no permanent record, what is recorded already is of a very vast and formidable quantity. The world of today is addressing itself to the complex problem of putting this available recorded information to proper use. Therefore, 'information' is understood today as almost synonymous with recorded information or documents. It is with this information that the librarians are directly concerned.

WHAT IS COMMUNICATION?

Wilbur Schramm (1972) says: "*There is a paradox about the term 'communication'; it is at once obvious and obscure. Its meaning seems to be obvious in contemporary usage but very elusive when we set out to capture its essence in a finely calibrated definition*". We know how to use the word 'communication' correctly. But we find it difficult to define the term 'communication'.

ETYMOLOGICAL EXPLANATION

'Communication' comes from the Latin term '*communicare*' which gives us an idea of 'sharing' and is related to other terms as 'communion' 'commune' and 'communist'. The term '*communis*' in Latin means 'common'. May be that when we communicate we are trying to establish a 'commonness' with some one, i.e. we are trying to share information, an idea or an attitude. The essence of communication is getting the receiver and the sender 'tuned' together for a particular message.

According to Lee Thayer (1963) who examined 20 definitions of the term 'communication' found that the link idea running through each of them is “the principle of social interaction through messages”; the concept of ‘message’ denoting a formally coded or symbolic event of shared significance.

Wilbur Schramm (1972) has emphasized the idea of the sharing and transmitting of meanings between individuals, a process fundamental to society in which the librarian plays a major role. Most textbooks on communication will attempt at some form of a definition of communication process, depending on the theoretical viewpoints of the authors. The work by Lee Thayer (1967) entitled “*Communication Concepts and Perceptions*” is a comprehensive work on the subject. He has discussed the definitions by psychologists, philosophers, neurologists, and other specialists. According to him these definitions generally tend to cohere into two main groups:

(a) The first group emphasizes the transfer of a mysterious something from the mind of one person to another, For example, *The Oxford English Dictionary* has defined: “*Communication, the imparting, conveying or exchanging of ideas, knowledge, etc, by means of speech, writing, or signs*”.

(b) The second group of definitions emphasizes the importance of human relationships and the social function of communication. For example, the Sociologist Charles Cooley in his “*Social organization* (1909) has summarized communication as: “*the mechanism by which all human relations exist and develop – all the symbols of the mind together with the means of conveying them through space and preserving them in time. These include expression of face, attitudes, gestures, tunes of voice, words, writing, printing, telegraph, telephones, and whatever else may be the latest achievement in the conquest of space and time*”. Cooley has conveyed his ideas as a sociologist on the function of communication in society. Another Sociologist, George Herbert Mead in his work *Mind Self and Society* (1934) , also has discussed this same idea. Claude E. Shannon (1949) has given the most comprehensive definition: "*The word communication will be used in a very broad sense to included all the procedures by which one mind may influence another. This involves not only written and oral speech, but also music, the pictorial arts, the theatre, the ballet, in fact all human behaviour...*".

In some connection it may be desirable to use a still broader definition of communication: namely, one which would include the procedure by which one mechanism say automatic equipment to track an airplane and compute its probable position, affects another mechanism, say a guided missile tracking the airplane. People can communicate among themselves with machines, and machines with other machines. The Shannon –Weaver (1949 definition has attempted to cover the whole repertoire of communication behaviour.

COMMUNICATION IN BIOLOGY

According to J.B.S. Haldane there are four classes of communication in biology: (1) between parts of the same cell; (2) between cells in the same organization; (3) between organisms of the same species; and (4) between organisms of different species. The most important signals used in communication are: (1) Chemical, (2) Optical, (3) Auditory, (4) Tactile, (5) Electrical, and (6) Others.

COMMUNICATION AS A PROCESS

A process is a sequence of events. The communication process is therefore a sequence of events, by which information is transferred from a source to a destination. This information may be either a signal, a stimuli or a symbol. In order to understand the communication process we use various devices to structure our thinking. These devices are called

Communication Models. Such models are the maps of the events which make up the communication process, or the flow charts showing how communication works. Such communication models are mainly due to the influence of electrical engineering and cybernetics upon what is known as communication theory. The idea of communication theory was first introduced by two classic works in the field, viz. (1) *Mathematical theory of communication* by Claude E. Shannon and Warren Weaver (1949) and *The Human Use of Human Beings: Cybernetics and Society* by Norbert Wiener (1950). We will go to these topics perhaps later.

HOW COMMUNICATION WORKS

Communication always require at least three elements: the Source, the Message, and the Destination. When we communicate we are trying to establish a commonness with someone, i.e. we are trying to share information, idea or an attitude. Now what happens when the source tries to establish this commonness with his intended destination?:

1. The source encodes the message, i.e. he takes the information or feeling he wants to share and puts it into a form that can be transmitted. For example, they are coded into spoken words, or written words.
2. In order to complete the act of communication the message must be decoded at the destination.

This process can be illustrated as follows:

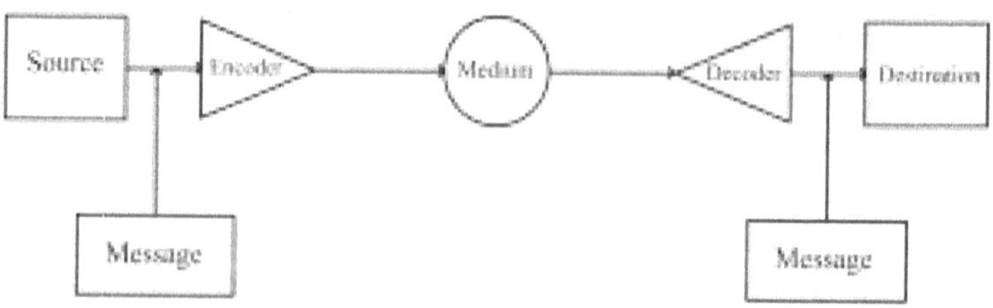

Fig. 4.1. Simple Model of How Communication Works

Suppose we apply this process to the electronic communication through radio or telephone:

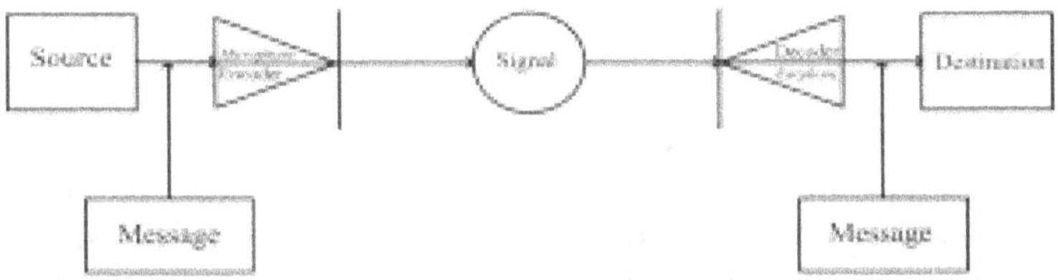

Fig. 4.2. Electronic Model of How Communication Works

Consider the source and encoder as one person, the decoder and destination as another person, and the signal as the language, we have then the process of human communication. In human communication something is very particular: once coded and sent, a message is quite free of its sender, i.e. the sender is not in a position to change, It is beyond his power to change the message already sent.

UNCERTAINTIES IN COMMUNICATION

There are many uncertainties as far as the sender is concerned:

1. Will it reach the destination?
2. Will he understand it as you intend him to?
3. Will he respond as you want him to? I e. Will the receiver be really in tune with the sender? – whether the message will be interpreted without distortion?

The most important thing about the communication process is that the sender and the receiver must be in tune with each other. In the case of a radio transmitter and receiver this maybe clear, but it is more complicated in human communication. The source can encode and the destination can decode only in terms of the experience each had. Examples:

1. If we have never learned any Russian, we can neither encode or decode in that language.

2. When non-science student tries to read Einstein.
3. The word 'dog" would be meaningless to a person who has not seen a dog or its picture – who comes from a dog-less island,
4. The word "dowry" does not convey the correct meaning to a Westerner.

This means that experience of source and destination have to be alike. if there is no common experience then the communication is impossible. The source has to encode in such a way as to make it easy for the destination to tune in the message – to relate it to parts of his experience which are much like those of the source. How this is done?

ROLE OF LANGUAGE IN COMMUNICATION

Messages are made of 'signs'. A sign is a signal that stands for something in experience, e.g. The word "dog"/ "goose" is such a sign which stands for our generalized experience with dogs/goose. We learn the signs by association. When we learned, it produced in us much the same response as the object stood for, although 'sign' is not the 'object'. There is difference between the 'sign' and the 'object'. Our messages are made up of signs, The sign system is merely a kind of shorthand. The coder has to be able to write the shorthand, the decoder to read it.

SIGNS, SYMBOLS AND MEANING

Language is the most powerful and basic tool in human communication. Language is the interplay of 'signs', 'symbols' and 'meaning' – the Trio. A 'sign' is something that stands for a referent (the object referred to by the 'sign'). So, a word is an 'artificial sign'. While rainwater on the side walk is a 'natural sign'. The red light at a traffic junction is a 'sign' or 'signal'. Others are 'smoke signal', 'telegraph signals', etc. Artificial signs can be 'verbal' (using words) or 'non-verbal' (expressions, hand shakes, etc.). Natural Signs are important to the survival of all animals.

DIFFERENCE BETWEEN 'SIGNS' AND 'SYMBOLS'

According to some there is no difference between 'signs' and 'symbols', while some others say there is difference. 'Signs' are used as proxy for objects: 'Symbols' are vehicles for conceptualizing the objects. When we think of something which is not present, 'signs' become 'symbols'. For example, the sign of a cross (+) represents Christianity; the sign of a lotus represents a particular political party. Sign of the cross (+) is represented by the word "cross". This is the process of symbolization. Symbol making is the basic need of man. It is the starting point for the origin of language.

Sensory data (what is perceived) is being shaped into symbols. The ability to use symbols is a source of power because ideas can be expressed beyond sensory data, like sight, sound, touch, smell and taste.

Meanings are in individuals. When we try to communicate with some one we are striving to use signs of symbols which will evoke similar meanings in that person.

SYMBOLIC INTERACTIONS

Meanings are relative. Different persons in different environments mean different things by the same symbols. Therefore, the society has to establish a more stable structure = established meanings for accepted symbols. Thus each language is a system of structurized signs, symbols and meanings.

COMMUNICATION MODELS

Communication Models are devices used to understand the communication process. A process is a sequence of events and a model can depict this sequence of events in a linear manner. As such communication model is a graphic illustration of the communication process. There are different models now available for illustrating the communication process. Every such model is a flow chart or map of events taking place in a communication process.

SHANNON AND WEAVER MODEL

The first communication model was developed by the Mathematician Claude E. Shannon in the late 1940s. This is still the most important and the one having widespread interest. Shannon was working in the Bell Telephone Laboratory and his model primarily applied to the field of telephonic communication. There he was concerned with the choice of the appropriate channel for transmitting the maximum amount of signals; and questions like how much of the transmitted signals will be destroyed by noise under way from transmitter to receiver. These are questions dealing with mainly the field of information theory. Nevertheless the graphical model made by Shannon and his co-worker Warren Weaver in 1949, has been used analogically by behavioural and linguistic scientists.

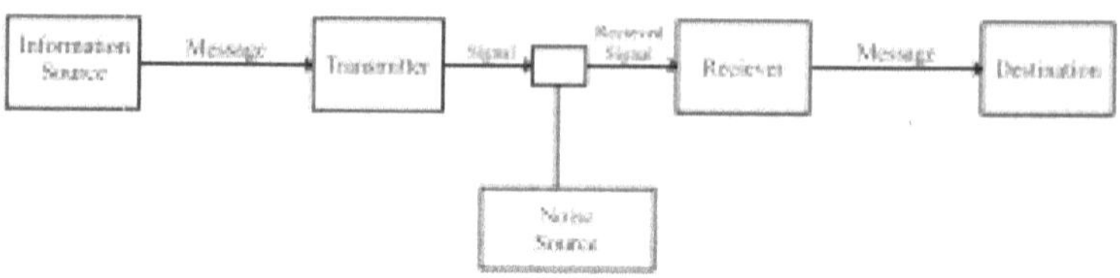

Fig. 4.3. A Linear Model of Communication Process by Shannon & Weaver, 1949

Shannon's model has influenced most of the later models. Communication is here described as a linear, one way process. According to Johnson and Klare (1961) *"of all single contributions to the wide spread interests of models today, Shannon' s is the most important because the technical side of communication research, Shannon's Mathematical formulations were the stimulus to much of the later efforts in this area.*

The mathematical aspects of Shannon's work is not discussed here, since he worked for the Bell Telephone Laboratory and his theories and models primarily applied to its particular field of Communication, involving questions, such as:

- Which kind of communication channel can bring through the maximum amount of signals?
- How much of transmitted signal will be destroyed by noise underway from transmitter to receiver?

These are questions mostly dealt with within the field of Information Theory. Nevertheless the graphical model, made by Shannon and his co-worker Warren Weaver (1949) ha s been used analogically by behavioural and linguistic scientists. Technological problems differ of course from human ones, but it is easy find the traces of Shannon-Weaver Model in a number of later models of human communication.

In Shannon's model communication is described as a linear, one way process. The model states five functions to be performed, namely Producing, Encoding, Transmitting, Receiving, and Decoding, and notes one dysfunctional factor, "Noise". Graphically, it may be presented as in Fig.1

First in the process is the Information *Source* producing *a message or a chain of messages* to be communicated. In the next step, the message is formed into *signals* by a transmitter. The signals should be adapted to the *channel* leading to the *receiver*. Thus the model depicts the acts of *Producing, Encoding, Transmitting, Receiving* and *Decoding*. The function of the receiver is the opposite of the transmitter. The receiver reconstructs the message from the signal. The received message then reaches the destination. The signal is vulnerable in so far as it may be disturbed by *Noise*. *Noise* is any Interference which may occur, for example, when there are many signals in the same channel at the same time. This may result in a difference between transmitted and received signals, which, in its turn may mean that the message produced by the source and that constructed by the receiver and having reached the destination do not have the same meaning. The inability on the part of communicators to realize that a sent and received message are not always identical, is a common reason why communication fails.

DE FLEUR'S MODEL

Melvin Lawrence De Fleur (1966) developed the Shannon and Weaver model further in a discussion about the correspondence between the meaning of the *produced* and *received* message. He notes that in communication process 'meaning' is so as to represent the Feed Back process. An information source may produce a message or a chain of messages to be communicated.

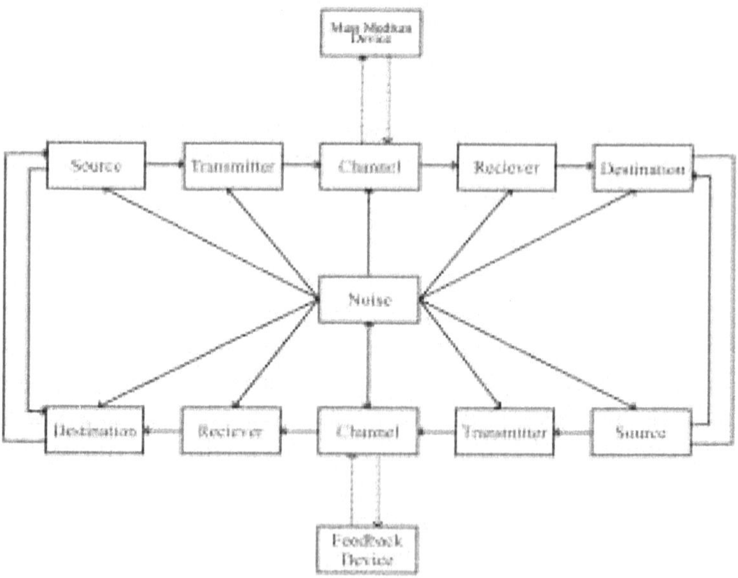

Fig. 4.4. De Fleur's Developed Model of Shannon and Weaver, Allowing Feedback

In the model De Fleur adds another set of components to the original Shannon and Weaver model to show how the source gets its feedback, which gives the source a possibility of adapting more effectively its way of communicating to the destination. This increased the possibility of achieving correspondence between the meanings at both ends. Shannon and Weaver model is thus supplemented in an important way by De Fleur.

OSGOOD AND SCHRAMM CIRCULAR MODEL

Charles Egerton Osgood was a distinguished American psychologist who developed a technique for measuring the connotative meaning of concepts known as the semantic differential. The Shannon Model could be described as linear, while this model by C.E. Osgood and Wilbur Schramm (1954) is highly circular. While Shannon was primarily interested in the channels between the **Sender** and **Receiver** Osgood and Schramm devote their discussion to the human behaviour of the actors in the communication process. Even then there are important similarities between the two approaches. While the Shannon-Weaver Model depicts communication as one-way process, the other models describe communication as an endless circular process.

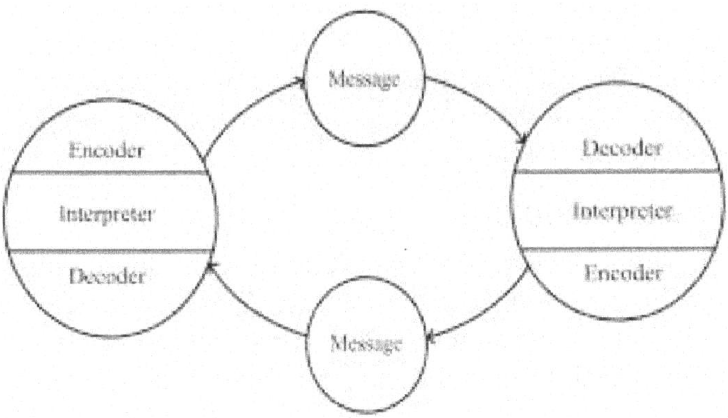

Fig. 4.5. Osgood & Shramm's Conversion Model of Communication

The various elements in this model are:

Message : the idea to be transferred.

Encoder : who does encoding or sends the message (message originates),

Decoder : Who receives the message,

Interpreter : Person trying to understand (analyse, preceive, or interpret),

From the message starting to ending, there is an interpretation goes on. Based on this interpretation only the message is received.

This model breaks the sender and receiver model as it seems communication in a practical way It It is not a traditional model.

It can happen within our self or between two peoples; each person acts as both sender and receiver and hence use interpretation. It is simultaneously taking place , e.g. encoding, interpreting and decoding. Semantic noise is a concept introduced here. It occurs when sender and receiver apply different meanings to the same message. It happens mostly because of words and phrases, for e.g. technical language. So certain words and phrases will cause you to deviate from the actual meaning of the communication.

Note : When semantic noise takes place decoding and interpretation becomes difficult and people get deviated from the actual message. This model does not talk about semantic noise and it assumes the moment of encoding and decoding.

LASSWELL MODEL

The American Political Scientist Harold D. Lasswell while he was a professor at Yale Law School in 1948 published his article that described an act of communication as answering the following questions:

Who

Says **What**

In which **channel**

To **whom**

With what **effect.**

These are the components of Lasswell's Communication Model. This has ever since been known and cited also as the Lasswell Formula. This can be transformed to a graphic model as in the diagram:

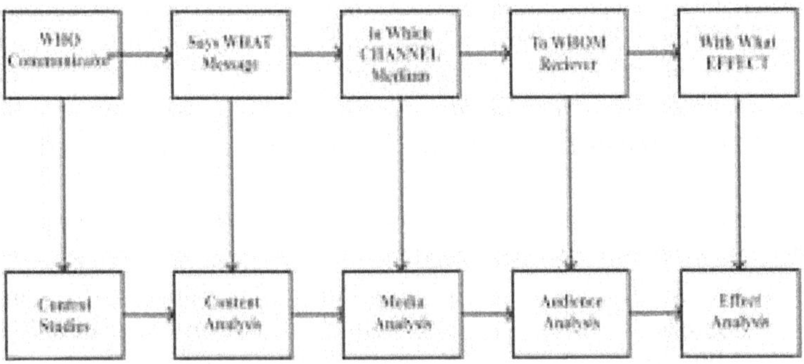

Fig. 4.6. Lasswell Formula with Corresponding Fields of Communication Research

Lasswell has later used this model to point out distinct types of communication research. To each question he has attached a particular type of analysis as is visualized in the Fig. 4.6.

REFERENCES

COOLEY, Charles Horton, Ed (1909). *Social Organisation; a study of the larger mind,* New York, Charles Scribners,The Mead Project.

DE FLEUR, M. L. (1966), De Fleur Model of Communication jose.wordpress.com by Dalu Jose 7 years ago.

DE FLEUR, Melvin Lawrence (1982), *Theories of Mass Communication,* Sandra Ball-Rokeach ,Longman,1982

GUPTA, B.L. (1987) : *Knowledge , Communication and Library* , Jaipur, Printwell, 1987.

HALDANE, J.B.S and HUXLEY, Julian (1927) *Animal Biology,* Oxford Clarendon, Google Scholar.

JOHNSON, F. Craig and KLARE, G. R., "General models of communication research: a survey of the developments of a decade", *Journal of Communication,* 1961.

LASSWELL, Harold D (1948),"The Structure and Function of Communication in Society: the Communication of Ideas" New York, *Institute for Religious and Social Studies,*p.117.

MEAD, George Herbert (1934), *Mind, Self and Society,* The definitive Edition, University of Chicago Press.

OSGOOD, Egerton and SCHRAMM , Wilbur(1954), "Osgood-Schramm Model of Communication: Definition and Application" in *Communication Models, Interpersonal Communication* (1954)

OXFORD ENGLISH DICTIONARY, First published in 1884, ed by James Murray.

SHANNON, Claude E. (1948) *The Mathematical Theory of Communication,* Bell Systems.

SHANNON, Claude E. and WEAVER, Warren (1949) *The Mathematical Theory of Communication* (1949), University of Illinois Press, WIENER, Norbert (1950) *The Human Use of Human beings; Cybernetics and Society* . Houghton Mifflin Harcourt, US.

SCHRAMM, Wilbur (1972), 'How communication works' *in* K. J. McGrarry *Mass Communication, selected readings for librarians.* Linnet Books, 1972 P.17.

THAYER, Lee (1963) "On Theory Building in Communication" in *Journal of Communication,* December 1963.

THAYER, LEE (1967), *Communication Concepts and Perspectives,* ERIC

VICKERY, Brian .C. and VICKERY, Alina (1987), *Information Science in theory and practice, Butterworths, 1987.*

5

History of Human Communication

Communication is, in the words of V.L.Narayana Menon (1976), "*access or means of access between two or more persons or places*". If so, the two facets of communication are: (a) access between individuals, and (b) means of access between individuals. In this division, the first represents communication proper, while the second denotes transportation. Hence there is the rationale in discussing often transport and communication together. However, the two needs to be surveyed separately.

Communication is basic to group life. The ability to communicate is found developed in varying degree in plants and animals. For example, among ants and bees group life, and hence communication, is more developed than in others. Animals do communicate mainly by visual, olfactory (smelling), and tactile (touching and feeling) signals to display emotions of fear, aggressiveness, and courtship. Vocal signals are the prerogative of the more highly evolved species. Man's achievement is that he makes a conscious rather than instinctual effort to communicate. It was this that led to the articulation of speech. In the process of evolution matter, life and mind is the order and it is with mind that intelligible communication is developed. Mind is available only with humans and hence in man only such communication has developed. Vocal signals are the prerogative of the more highly evolved species. They are accidental. Man's achievement is that he makes a conscious rather than instinctual effort to communicate. It was this that led to the articulation of speech.

NON-VERBAL COMMUNICATION

Man has been trying to communicate more and more effectively in course of time. The human species must have spent several millenniums trying to communicate with members of the same species. Crying, grunting, roaring, laughing, gesticulating, etc, were the initial efforts. Out of these efforts must have evolved in a slow measure emerged sounds which were identified with objects, animals and trees, and actions of all kinds, thoughts, deeds and feelings. Thus the spoken word was formed as the most valuable instrument that man ever created - as a combination of sound, symbol and meaning. This new mode of communication must have grown and refined to the limit of man's capacity over a long period of time, depending on man's environments, his needs, his physical features, etc. Speech took on different sounds, different pronunciations, and stresses and accents in the different nooks and corners of this wide world. Thus different dialects and languages were formed.

THE SPOKEN WORD

We do not know when man began to talk? Which community started it and where? We do not know anything of the past until recorded history began. But we know for certain that the world of the spoken word had reached some perfection, before writing began. The earliest classics, great epics, pronouncements, dialogues, etc. belonging to the days before the invention of writing, which has been passed on to us by word of mouth, through oral communication, and finally preserved by the word, like the wisdom of Socrates, or the *Upanishads* of India, or the *Iliad* of Homer or the narratives in *Genesis* (Bible) — are clues to this knowledge. They all show that languages were already in a state of almost perfection. Thus we had a strong oral tradition of knowledge.

INVENTION OF WRITING

Then came the invention of writing. Writing gave the spoken word a visual shape. There was a long period of human history before writing was invented. And it took a longer period for writing to become common heritage. Primary reasons for the origin of writing were (a) communication (c) religion and (c) economic (Otto Jesperson,1938). Writing facilitated recording of messages meant for distantly situated individuals. It served religious purpose of recording prayers, mantras, and procedures for worship where consequences of errors or mistakes were deemed fatal. It also served economic purpose of creating and preserving rightful authority of ownership of properties, like title deeds, records of economic and commercial transactions, agreements and treaties.

The Canadian philosopher Marshall McLuhan (1964) wrote: "*Until writing was invented man lived in acoustic space; boundless, directionless, horizonless, in the dark of the mind, in the world of emotion, by primordial intuition, by terror. Speech is the social chart of this boy. The goose quill put an end to talk. It abolished mystery; it gave architecture and towns, it brought roads and armies, bureaucracy. It is the basic metaphor with which the cycle of civilization began, the step from the dark into the light of the mind. The hand that filled the parchment page built a city*".

First attempts at graphic communication were the rude scratching found on rocks and cave walls. Clans who habituated and passed by forest areas gave markings on trees and stones they came across. Pictures were made on to the walls using carbon or vegetable pastes. Such works are done probably 10,000 to 15,000 years ago. The drawings on caves of Southern France and Spain, for example, are dated roughly 10,000 B.C. and are elaborate and realistic, using earth colours and animal fat. Another species of old records are the Marked Colour Stones, for example the *Azilian Pebbles* found in Southern France. Yet another item is the Mnemonic Devices used by primitive people like *Quipus* or Knotted Chords. The *Wampum* (=belt of beads) of the North American Indians and the *Clog Almanac* (=a notched stick of wood) of European peasants in the middle ages are there now as illustrative examples.(Elmer D. Johnson, 1960).

Writing proper was developed over the ages through successive stages of *Pictographs*, *Ideographs* and *Phonograms*. Pictographs are pictures of objects like men, animals, sun, etc. Ideographs conveyed a meaning other than the thing depicted, like sun for day light. The Egyptian Pictographs with established phonetic values are the *Heiroglyphics* used for sacred carvings by Egyptians was a pictographic writing as old as 4000 B.C. Egyptians and Babylonians used ideographs in the beginning which they advanced to the stage of Phonogram where a pictorial symbol took on a particular sound, and conveyed that sound meaning although the pictorial meaning might be different. For example is the picture of a bee to represent the verb "be" and the picture of bee and a leaf to mean "belief".

DEVELOPMENT OF SCRIPTS

It was later that various scripts began to be formed. The *Cuneiform Script* was developed by the Sumerian-Babylonian and Assyrian civilization. It was the

Phoenicians who first used the Phonetic Alphabet of 22 letters around 900 B.C. The Greek took up the phonetic alphabet from Phoenicians and adopted it to their own language and used it to create a great literature. From the Greeks the alphabet passed to the Romans who in course of time developed the present alphabet of 26 letters.

WRITING MATERIALS USED

Stone was evidently the first material surface used for writing. These writings were known as *inscriptions*. Stone was heavy and could not be handled easily. Almost simultaneously softer surfaces like Clay Tablets and Cylinders began to be used in the Mesopotamian civilization. Almost in the same period papyrus rolls began to be widely used by Egyptians while Hebrews and Persians chose animal skins to make their Parchment and Vellum codex. In India Palm Leaf was in wider use although barks and leaves of trees were also used. Thus at the dawn of history, every civilized nation is discovered to have been in possession of a system of book making, each having selected materials made accessible by its surroundings. Commensurate with the choice of material surfaces a script system suitable for writing on that surface was also developed like for example the *cuneiform* (wedge shaped) script for carving on harder surfaces like stone, *hieroglyphics* for writing on softer materials like papyrus sheets or parchment and vellum.

INVENTION OF PAPER

Paper was invented in China in 105 A.D.by T'Sai Lun as a relatively cheap commodity which could be produced on relatively mass scale. He experimented old fishnets and other cotton waste which was soaked in water to be spread out as sheets to give the body of paper. Later, more materials were used to give the carbohydrate cellulose necessary for the paper. Thus cotton rags, wood pulp, bamboo and other grasses, etc. formed the source material for paper. By 12th century, paper replaced every other writing material and it began to be produced from wood pulp by factory based system for manufacturing paper in bulk.

DEVELOPMENT OF PRINTING

Like the manufacture of paper Printing also was invented first in China. The successive stages of development in the art and technique of printing were (a) Picture printing, (b) Printing of block books, and (c) printing from moveable types. The Buddhist Charms of 5th/6th century are extant specimens of earliest picture printing done in China. In the 9th century experiments were common with printing of carved texts on blocks of wood and the outstanding example was *Diamond Sutra* printed as a complete block book with a certain date of printing on it like "printed 11th May 868 by Feng Tao" (Elmer D. Johnson,1960). Experiments on carving individual types suited to printing books were found impractical due to the peculiar nature of the Chinese language with its numerous letters and characters. Eventually, printing from moveable types was first accomplished in Europe, in Mainz, Germany by Jonathan Gutenberg in the year 1456 and his first complete work was the *Gutenberg Bible* (42-line Bible). Gutenberg gave two essential developments in printing, firstly he developed a type metal with an alloy of led and antimony. Until then wood was used as the type material. He developed the technique of printing with a printer's ink which was oil based whereas until then printer's ink was water-based.

Printing was further developed by William Caxton in England who established his Caxton Press as a commercial enterprise opening up the vista for book publishing business. The invention and development of printing put an end to the Middle Ages which was considered to be "Dark Ages". Printing of pamphlets and broadsheets became very popular in Germany during the

Reformation period. Printing was so far done from flat surfaces, the block being made of *relief printing, planography* and *intaglio* processes. In 1813 Friederich Koenig a German printer in London produced the first cylinder press where paper began to be fed into the flat bed by using a cylinder. In 1814, the newspaper the London Times augmented the Koenig Press with a steam engine which increased the speed of execution. Almost immediately, the use of stereotype plates was introduced which enabled the making of cervical printing plates. In 1830s saw the use of assembly line method of printing, folding, stitching and binding, making possible the production of books and pamphlets at a much higher speed. In 1846 Richard M. Hoe in USA developed the Rotary Press almost increasing the speed of production to 8,000 impressions per hour, enabling the continuous feeding of paper from a roll. This was soon followed by the development of electrotype plate which enabled the reproduction of pictures with more clarity. The Rotary Press was further developed into Web-fed Press in 1865 by William Bullock in USA.

Despite the developments in printing methods, type setting by hand still continued for long. In the 1820s William Church designed and constructed a machine for setting types mechanically from a hand operated key board. The idea was perfected after several improvements, in the 1885 by Ottmar Mergenthaler under the patent name of Linotype, a machine operated from a key-board, similar to a typewriter and cast in one piece a complete line of type. The Linotype was first used by the New York Tribune in 1886 (Johnson, 1960).

The invention of photography gave further stimulus to the art and technique of printing and book making, which was done by Niepice in France in 1826, and Fox Talbot in UK in 1835 and John Corbett in USA in 1888. The photo-offset printing process which was developed finally in US in 1904 by Ira Washington Rubel had the advantages of reproducing both picture and text at the same time, and also of printing on cheaper paper and this technique in effect revolutionized modern printing. Narayana Menon (1976) remarked:" *We don't often realize the changes that techniques of communication cause in social behavior, in attitudes in general. A new technology in communication is not merely a new way of communicating thoughts ideas, information. It creates a new way of life, a new kind of man*".

OTHER DEVELOPMENTS IN COMMUNICATION

Two important developments in communication are worth recording. They were the telegraph and the wireless telegraph. Telegraph is the long-distance transmission of textual messages where the sender uses symbolic codes known to the recipient, rather than a physical exchange of an object bearing the message. Having been invented in the late 18th century it was widely used in France and European countries during the Napoleonic era. The electric telegraph started to replace the optical telegraph in the mid- 19th century. It began to be widely used in railway signaling in the United States. This was supplemented by the Morse System of Samuel Morse in 1865 in Germany (*en.m.wikipedia.org*). The telephone was patented in the name of Alexander Graham Bell in US in1876. In 1901 wireless telegraphy became possible and the first time Trans-Atlantic call was made from US to UK by Guglielmo Marconi.

About 500 years after printing, Radio burst upon us, making communication possible on a mass basis. Canadian Reginald A Fessenden is credited to have used the modulation radio waves which allowed the reception and transmission of the voice on the same aerial without interference. In 1915 speech was transmitted across the continent from New York to San Francisco and across Atlantic Ocean from Naval Station at Virginia to the Eiffel Tower in Paris. The Marconi Station in Chelmsford came into existence in 1920 with daily two programmes broadcasting which later became the BBC. In America also efforts were made towards broadcasting and by 1924 there were about 500 stations in the country, and the Commercial radio telephone linking North America with Europe was opened in 1927, and in 1935 the first telephone call was made around the world using a combination of wire and radio circuits. Radio reached peak popularity with general audiences in the 1930s and 1940s. Hardly 40 years has passed after the invention and perfection of the valve we found a substitute for it, smaller, more compact, cheaper, the ubiquitous transistor. and the Commercial radio telephone linking North America with Europe was opened in 1927, and in 1935 the first telephone call was made around the world using a combination of wire and radio circuits. In the words of Narayana Menon (1976) "*Radio could present the world to the whole world. It made the dissemination of news, of information, of comment, of entertainment possible on a scale unprecedented in human history. The spoken word was rehabilitated with its full force – or nearly full force. And just as the supremacy of sound was being accepted as the key factor in communication, television overtook it; the visual element asserting itself again. All this in one's life time.*" In India the first broadcasting station was started in Bombay in 1927, the second in Calcutta. The Government took over the service in 1935 and renamed it All India Radio.

The story of television started in 1924 when John Baird experimented on transmitting. In 1927, the first electronic Television was invented by Philo Taylor Farnsworth. He used technology called a Cathode Ray Tube (CRT) as well as two or more anodes. Already from 1907 other inventors, were experimenting on a mechanical television system. By 1934 all the mechanical television systems in use were converted into the electronic system of Farnsworth. World's first television stations started in

America in the late 1920s. The first television station, aired its first broadcast on July 2, 1928 when the America's first television programme called the Queen's Messenger was shown. Television in the beginning was only in black and white while Colour Television began to be popular during the 1950s only.. According to Nayarana Menon, (1983) "in 1981 there were about 583 million TV sets in the world of which 157 million were in the USA and 144 million in Western Europe". Television has today become an intricate part of our everyday lives, exerting its influences both good and bad.

THE INTERNET AND THE SOCIAL MEDIA

Almost soon after the advent and popularity of the Television has come the IT revolution wherein the computer technology and communication science joined hands giving birth to an Internet culture. Two important events in history of Information Technology are worth recording, one on 29th October 1969 the *ARPAnet* the precursor of the Internet was established in the University of California, and the other about two years later, i.e. in March 1989 Tim Berners-Lee proposed the *World Wide Web.* These two events in the digital age, one a network infrastructure, the other (the Web) a software infrastructure layered on top of it. More than a third of the world's population was connected by the network benefitting the use by millions of people. As on 2017, (*en. Wikipedia.org/wiki/history of the Internet*) there was an estimated 3.9 million Internet users word wide. This accounts for more than half of the global population, with China having the biggest online population (829 millions) followed by India (560 millions), and the US (293 millions). By 2021 there will be over 600 million Internet users in India, despise the fact that only 17 per cent of Indian population only use Internet in 2015.

As a consequence of the Internet revolution came the advent and spread of the Social Media. "*Social media are interactive computer-mediated technologies that facilitate the creation or sharing of information, ideas, career interests, and other forms of expression via virtual communities and networks*" (*en-wikipedia.org/wiki/Social- Media*).

In 2019 *Merriam –Webster* dictionary defined Social Media as "*forms of electronic communication (such as websites for social networking and micro-blogging) through which users create online communities to share information, ideas, personal messages, and other content such as videos*"(*https://www.merriam-webster.com).* The earliest form of the Internet was CompuServe developed in 1960 whereas the first recognizable Social Media site, *Six Degrees* was created in 1997 only.

According to *Statistica* 2019 it is estimated that there will be around 2.77 billion Social Media users around the globe, up from 2.46 billion in 2107. Most poplar Social Networks are : Facebook (2,375 miilions), YouTube (2,000 millions), WhatApp (1,600 millions), Facebook Messenger (1,300 millions) WeChat (1,112 millioons), Instagram (1,000 millions), Twitter (330 million). LinkedIn (310 millions) and Pinterest (265 millions).

There are some common features for Social Media, (1) They are interactive Web 2.0 Internet based applications; (2) User-generated content such texts, posts or comments, digital photos or videos, and data generated through online interactions is the lifeblood of social media; (3) Users create specific profiles and identities for the website or apps that are designed and maintained by the social media organizations; and (4) Social Media facilitate the development online social networks by connecting a user's profile to those of other individuals or groups. Users at first started accessing social media services via web-based apps/technologies on desktops and laptops, but soon they switched over to Smart Phones and Tablets, the surge in the production and sale of Smart Phones further promoted the use of Social Media. Social Media outlets operate in a dialogic transmission system (=many sources to many receivers), in contrast to the traditional media which operates under a mono-logic transmission model (=one source to many receivers).

TRANSPORTATION

Now, let us take a look at the growth of communication in another sense – means of access between two or more places. For about two million years, until hundred and fifty years ago, mankind was confined to the speed of a galloping horse, about 30miles per hour. The message carrying pigeon, i.e. the pigeon post, and the introduction of the message carrying postal system were the fulfillments in communication between distantly situated persons. An enormous step forward was the discovery of the wheel which changed the very concept of movement and travel. Emperor Augustus who reigned between 27BC and 14 AD is reported to have established the first official postal service. Himself and his successors built 47,000 miles of well engineered roads that covered the empire as well as many relay stations to facilitate their horse drawn mail carts where relay teams could travel about 50 miles a day could easily carry and deliver messages. The discovery of the trade routes opened up trade and commerce with different parts of the world. This was followed by the locomotive and the steam engine. The railways opened up the vast vista of land and space practically all around the world at a higher speed and with more comforts.

The telegraph was perfected much about the same time as the locomotive in the mid-nineteenth century. The steam engine did a lot of things and was the crucial and central motive power for communications with trans-continental, international coverage. And then almost suddenly came the internal combustion engine which meant the emergence of the automobile and the car rush where by the middle of the 20th century even lower middle class families owned a car. This led to the creation more roads, and macadamizing or concreting the available ones. Enormous, long and powerful trucks took over the cargo transport. In the mean time the internal combustion engine had created aviation leading to the operation of large trans-continental planes which could transport you right across oceans and over the highest mountains at 300 miles an hour. Then came the Jet engine. A single jumbo-jet could transport ore passenger across the Atlantic in a week than the biggest boats could. We have broken the sound barrier and can really and truly beat the clock. One can leave London at 10 a.m., arrive New York same day after a 3,000 miles flight at 9 a.m. As we triumph over distances, we get enslaved with devices which become imperative to sustain the triumph. The physical means of communicating information, messages and news have gone hand in hand. Car drivers used radios, stereos, etc. Aeroplanes were not allowed to operate without wireless, and ships cannot sail without it. The faster, the more refined our means of travel, the more sophisticated, the more effective our means of communicating with the world would be. Distances shrink, national barriers disappear, and we are a global village - all these changes happened in less than a century.

MAJOR EVENTS IN HUMAN COMMUNICATION

The Spoken Word

- As a combination of sound, symbol and meaning.
- Formation of different dialects and languages.

The Written Word

- Primitive graphic communications; cave painting (From 10,000 to 15,000 years ago).
- Use of various mnemonic devices
- Quipus or Knotted Chords of the Peruvians;
- Wampum or Belt of Beads of North American Indians.

- the Pictographs of the North American Indians; and peoples of Africa, South America and Asia.
- the Ideographs developed by Egyptians and Babylonians.
- the Phonogram developed by Egyptians.
- the Phonetic Alphabet developed by the Phoenicians and later took over by the Greek.
- the use of various writing materials - Stone, Backed Clay, Papyrus, Parchment, Palm Leaves, etc.

105 AD - Invention of Paper in China by T'Sai Lun.

The Printed Word

- Picture printing in China in the 5th Cy AD.
- Printing of block books in China in the 9th Cy AD.
- Printing of books from moveable types - early experiments in China.
- Printing from moveable types by Johannes Gutenberg in Germany in 1450s

1456 A.D.- The 42-line Gutenberg Bible.

1529 The First Newspaper type of Broadsheet.

1622 The First Periodical "*the Weekly News*" was published by Nathaniel Butler.

1702 Printing of *Daily Courant* the first daily paper in England.

1799 Development of Lithography for block printing.

1814 Use of steam-operated printing press by the *Times* in London.

1840s Invention and Development of Telegraphy.

1845 The Rotary Press was perfected by Richard Hoe.

1858 Laying of the first Trans-Atlantic Cable.

1876 Alexander Graham Bell and Thomas Watson exhibit an electric telephone.

1877 Thomas Edison patents the phonograph.

1895 Invention of Wireless by Marconi.

1901 Marconi transmitted Radio Signals.

1920 The Opening of the first Radio Station in Pittsburgh.

1923 The Appearance of the Television; Picture televised between New York and Philadelphia.

1940s Development of the Electronic Computers – the First Generation computers, Mark I, ENIAC, etc.

1941 Full Commercial Television.

1948 The Development of Transistors.

1959 The Use of Transistors in the Second Generation Computers.

1965 The Third Generation Computers with miniaturized circuits.

1970 The Fourth Generation Computers with large scale integration and miniaturization.

REFERENCES

en. Wikipedia.org/wiki/history of the Internet.

en-wikipedia.org/wiki/Social- Media.

https://www.merriam-webster.com.

JESPERSON, Otto (1938), *Growth and structure of the English Language,* Rev Edn Read Books Ltd, 2011.

JOHNSON, Elmer D. (1960). *Communication; an introduction to the history of the alphabet, writing, printing, books and libraries,* Edn.2. The Scarecrow Press, New York.

McLUHAN, Marshall (1964): *The Medium Is the Message: An Inventory of Effects,* Penguin Modern Classics.

NARAYANA MENON, V.K. (1976), *The Communication Revolution,* New Delhi, National Book Trust of India.

UNESCO (1981) *Many Voices One World (MacBride Commission Report); Communication and Society ; Today and Tomorrow,* Roman & Littlefield Publishers.

Statistica quarterly journal (ISSN 1973-2201) Vol.79(No.4) 2019.

6

Properties and Behaviour of Information

The basic areas of Information Science were identified as follows:

(a) Information as a phenomenon –its properties and behavior;

(b) Communication process and the transmission of information; and

(c) Information Systems as mechanisms by means of which communication process is realized.

According to William Goffman (1970), "*Information Science aims at being a unified approach to the study of the various phenomena connected with the notion of information*". The basic thing, therefore is to study what is 'information'.

Information is a very nebulous concept – although intuitively understood cannot be formally defined. Most dictionaries have attempted to define information as knowledge, intelligence, facts, or data which can be used, transferred or communicated. But a closer study of the concept of information will reveal that it is not equal to knowledge. We will learn about how information is different from knowledge later.

As Klaus Otten (1974) has rightly put it, we talk about information with the belief that we know what information is, but when we try to define information we find that there is a variety of apparently fitting statements, although none is universally valid. The many definitions available reflect only subject and context dependant concepts. According to Debons and Cameron (1973), "one foremost problem facing the development of a science of information is the uncertainty as to what constitutes information".

DATA, INFORMATION, AND KNOWLEDGE

In the words of Manfred Kochen (1967),"*Information is decision-relevant data*". According to Whittenmore & Yovits (1972), "*Information is data of value to decision making*". Data may be considered signs, usually recorded observations, that are not currently affecting behavior. However, data become information if behaviour becomes affected. For example, the massive data contained in a computer database are only signs that are not affecting behaviour. Until the data are actually viewed, and are properly organized for a person who reacts to them, they are not information. Information is the net value obtained from the process of matching the elements of a present problem with approximate elements of data. (You may see also the discussion of the DIKW Pyramid in chapter 1 of this book).

INFORMATION INTO KNOWLEDGE

'Information' and 'knowledge' are not synonymous terms. Information may lead to knowledge. It is the precursor of knowledge.

There are logical, philosophical, and biological explanations for knowledge.

The biological interpretation of knowledge is advanced by people like R.F.A. Hoerule (1952). The logical interpretation of Knowledge is given by People like, John Dewey (1938). The growth process of knowledge is analogous to the growth process of organisms (Paul Weiss, 1964). The growth process in knowledge is comparable to the growth process in higher animals. As the growth of the latter is caused by the intake of food stuffs, from the environment through a process of degradation, screening, recombination, and synthesis, information is raw data collected from experience, which is analyzed, sorted, correlated, and conceptualized to become finally the part of existing knowledge. (You may see the discussion of this topic in chapter 1 of this book).

The epidemic model of the spread of scientific ideas as manifested in publications is demonstrated by Goffman and Newill (1964). According to this communication of ideas by recorded discourse is assumed to be governed by processes formally equivalent to communication of diseases by micro organisms and of signals by machines (You may see discussion of this topic in chapter 1 of this book).

NATURE, PROPERTIES AND BEHAVIOUR OF INFORMATION

What is a Property? A property is a characteristic or quality or attribute that is inherent or associated with an entity. For example are elasticity of rubber and porosity of sponge. In like manner information as a phenomenon has 3 sets of properties originally identified by communication engineers. They derive from each of the three aspects of information in the context of communication, plus other aspects. They are: (1) Physical,

(2) Semantic, (3) Behavioural, and (4) Other Social properties.

Physical properties relate to the body of the recorded information or document. Human communication can be oral or written, verbal or non-verbal, and also manual or mechanical. In the case of Recorded Information physical properties correspond with the variety of documents. They cover all items like archives, manuscripts, printed books, periodicals, and other items of printed documents, pictures, photographs, drawings, paintings, sound recordings, audio & video cassettes, cinematographic films, computer readable records like tapes, diskettes, hard disks, CD ROMS, etc, and Micrographics, like micro-card, micro-fiche, micro-films, etc.

Semantic properties correspond with the language and form of expression of the document involved. There can be natural language documents as well as artificial language documents like Braille books. There can be further groupings based on various literary forms, like prose, poetry, drama, fiction, etc, in every language.

Behavioural properties are caused by the incidents of the humans involved at either ends of the communication process, namely the Sender and the Receiver and all human intermediaries. In the case of the recorded information they include documents produced by special groups for the use of special groups. Every incident of communication is to be analyzed as to WHO says WHAT to WHOM. Sources of information and targeted audiences may vary from individuals, institutions, organizations, governments, etc. Documents can be written for children or adults, for beginners or advanced students, or for pedestrian readers.

Economic Property is the most significant in the case of all other properties of information. Information these days is reckoned as a commodity; which can be attributed value, utility, certainty, etc.

Other properties: Besides all human behavioural aspects, the Recorded Information show some special behavioural patterns like:

Accretion /growth

Scattering and seepage

Variety/Difference

Rarity

Redundancy / Duplication

Obscurity

Overload

Life/Perishabilty/Obsolescence

Pollution

Utility

Value – Uncertainty/Unpredictability

Indivisibility

Inappropriability

Some of these concepts have been discussed elsewhere in this book (See Chapter 11).

According to Charles M. Weiseman (1985), Information has several basic qualities like: existence, availability, language & meaning.

According W.F. Williams (1965) there are 6 parameters for information:

Quantity of information which cane measured by the number of documents, pages, words, characters, bits, drawings, pictures, etc;

Content, standing for the meaning of the information; *Structure,* meaning the format or organization of the information and its logical relationship or coherence between statements or elements;

Language, standing for the symbols, alphabets, codes, and syntax with which the ideas are expressed;

Quality, that which characterizes the completeness, accuracy, relevance, and timeliness of information; and

Life, meaning the total span of time in which value can be derived from information.

From the User's point of view, Information should have:

1. Novelty,
2. Recency/Timeliness,
3. Relevance/Pertinence/Utility,
4. Reliabitllity/Authenticity,
5. Content,
6. Structure
7. Coherence
8. Clarity
9. Completeness/Comprehensiveness,
10. Accessibility, and
11. Practicability.

GROWTH RATE OF PUBLICATIONS

In 1911 Iwinski estimated that here were then 25 million different books in the world. This number was arrived at after excluding the different editions, reprints, issues, variant copies, etc. of the same book, and all occasional, fugitive, ephemeral items as maps, charts, prints, proclamations, music, engravings, newssheets, newspapers, etc. (Details are found in *Bowker Annual)*. It has been estimated that in the firsts 500 years since Gutenberg (1454 A.D.) some 30 million printed books were published in the world. In the next 25 years an equal number was published (Dyer & Goldstein, 1970), about 5 lakhs to one million books every year. As on 5th August, 2010 Google estimated that there is nearly 130 million books published in the entire world (*http://mashable.com>2010/08/2010*). At an average 2-3 articles are published in over 100,000 periodicals in Science &

Technology alone. Over 50,000 to 1 million articles and patents on Chemistry are abstracted by Chemical Abstracts Services.

AGEING AND OBSOLESCENCE OF PUBLICATIONS

How far is the useful life of a document? - The decay or obsolescence rate of documents can be studied on an empirical basis in specific subject areas. However, it is generally found that fast growing subjects would have lesser longevity compared to others.

DISPERSION OR SCATTERING OF SUBJECTS

Scattering of information has been demonstrated in detail by S. C. Bradford (1948), who has also brought out the Law of Scattering. Later, Eugene Garfield (1971) who studied the trend of subject concentration has brought out his Law of Concentration. For a detailed discussion on these topics see Chapter 9 of this book. Some of the significant conclusions made from similar studies are that:

- Social Sciences and Art subjects show a wider scatter of publications than the Sciences.
- Research publications in Technology show a greater dispersion than those in Sciences.
- A new branch of Science, especially an interdisciplinary one, shows a greater dispersion than older branch of Science.

REFERENCES

BOWKER ANNUAL

BRADFORD, S.C. (1948); *Documentation*, London, Crosby Lockwood & Sons, 1948

DEBONS, A and CAMERON, J, Eds. "Editorial Summary" *in* Perspectives of Information Science, the proceedings of the II NATO Advanced Study Institute, Wales, 1973.

DEWEY, John (1938): *Logic, the theory of enquiry*, New York, Henry Hall & Co, 1938.

DYER, Christopher and GOLDSTEIN, Darwin (1970): *School*

libraries, theory and practice, Bingley, 1970

GARFIELD, Eugene (1971): "The mystery of the Transposed Journal Lists, wherein Bradford's Law of Scattering is generalized according to Garfield's Law of Concentration" *Current Contents*, 31 (1971): 5-6.

GOFFMAN, W. and NEVILLE, V.A. (1964) "A General Theory of Communication", ("Epidemic Theory of Communication; Epidemic model of the spread of scientific ideas as manifested by publication") *in* SARACEVIC, Tefko (1970), *Introduction to information Science*, Pp 726- , R.R. Bowker & Co, 1970.

HOERULE, R.F.A. *Studies in Philosophy*, London, Allen & Thomas, 1952. *http://mashable.com>2010/08/2010*

IWINSKI, Boleslas (1911): "The Heritage of Boleslas Iwinski"S *in Library Trends* 62(2):456-464, September 2013.

KOCHEN, Manfred (1967): Growth of Knowledge, New York, Wiley.

OTTEN, Klaus W. (1974): "Basis for a science of information" *in* Debons, Ed. *Information Science, search for identity*, p.91-100, New York, Marcel Dekker, 1974.

PARKER and PAISELEY *in* Tefko Saracevic: *Introduction to Information Science* Page 85-92.

WEISMAN, Charles M. (1985), *Strategic Information Systems*, McGraw-Hill Professional, 1985.

WEISS, Paul (1964): "Knowledge a growth process" *in* Manfred Kochen, Ed. *The growth of knowledge* N.Y., John Wiley,1964.

WHITTE, Bruce J. and YOVITS, M.C. (1974): "The quantification and analysis of information used in decision processes" *in Information Sciences*, 7:171-184, December 1974.

WHITTENMORE, B. J. & YOVITS, M.C. (1972), *A Generalized Conceptual Development for the Analysis and Flow of Information*, Ohio State University, Computer and Information Science Research Center, 1972.

WILLIAMS, Williams F. (1965): *Principles of Automated Information Retrieval (www.lisbdnet.com/parameters-of-information-for-education*).

7
Pattern of Scientific Communication

Communication is the essence of science and technology; it is the social process through which experts establish their claims to reliable knowledge about the natural world. Besides, there is the communication with the public including popular science writings, media coverage of science subjects, and the effects of public communication of science and technology on other social institutions. Over and above these, there are issues involving communication among scholars such as open-access publishing, digital libraries and other "expert information" topics, and public debates about emerging technologies. Science communication is the practice of informing, educating, sharing wonderment and raising awareness of science related topics. It may generate support for scientific research or study, or to inform decision making, including political and ethical thinking. Science communication is part of a scientist's everyday life. Scientists must give talks, write papers, communicate with a variety of audiences, and educate others. Among organized measures of scientific information besides the scientists, Librarians and Information Specialists are having significant roles to play.

Only in the recent decades the librarian or information specialist began to play a substantial role in scientific communication. Before that, scientists themselves were engaged in organizing the flow of information from the generator to the user. They depended on libraries only to the extent of getting physical access to the printed word. Instead, they devised their own methods of circulating information generated by them and of disseminating and retrieving the references of such publications. Such methods were different and there was a growing complexity because new methods did not replace the old ones but only added to them.

INFORMAL COMMUNICATION

Groups of scientists have built up informal, but sometimes elaborate, systems for the exchange of information through letters, mailing lists, conference schedules, and reprints. These groups are known as "the Invisible colleges". Through the "invisible colleges" and other informal means, a high proportion of scientific information was disseminated before formal publication. Most of the researchers are in the habit of communicating to their peers first by announcing research, and then publishing papers in formal journals. Colleagues take this research and extend or modify it. But there are some groups that communicate far more personally and regularly than this, using only informal channels. These groups comprise of the Elites of that branch of knowledge. De Solla Price (1963) has termed such groups of Elite Researchers "INVISBLE COLLEGES". An invisible college will comprise of the most well known and respected researchers, who know one another well and communicate each other often. Visibility is a measure of the extent to which members of the scientific community are acquainted with a scientist's work. Price suggested that the invisible college group would be higher producers in terms of number of papers, and that communication between members of this group would be crucial, and at the forefront of research area. The external contacts or communication links which form the backbone of an invisible college can be made and reinforced by attending conferences and meetings, exchanging letters and telephone calls, and by joining professional societies.

INFORMATION EXCHANGE GROUPS

Informal Invisible Colleges get almost formalized or an extension of the practice as Information Exchange Groups. Between 1961 and 1971 the National Institute of Health (U.S.) had set up a number of informal Information Exchange Groups. The idea was to utilize the concept of an Invisible college by streamlining communication and dissemination between a small group of scientists in a highly defined subject area. Members disseminated information by sending it to a local centre or a branch headquarters, and from there it was copied and sent round to all members within about a weak. The rapid speed of dissemination to a group with high information need meant that Information Exchange Groups were in no way the most successful arrangement. However, the selectivity of the group and lack of trust among some members of the group, have led to problems, and the Informal Exchange Group programme was wound up in 1967, due to lack of resources and because of rising criticism from traditional publishing channels. However, external contacts were established between individuals attending conferences, meetings, etc. through exchange of letters, telephone calls and membership in professional societies.

PRIMARY PUBLICATIONS

Formal publication of any original work is generally called "Primary Publications". They consist mainly of journal articles, and research reports, and to a lesser extent theses, monographs, and conference proceedings. At first, the scientific journals were published mainly by scientific societies but later governments and commercial publishers share them almost equally. These journals are published in many countries and languages and differ widely in quality, subject coverage, etc. Publishing in Primary Journals has the advantage that it is controlled and easily accessible through bibliographical guides. But, with regard to other publications the situation is different. They are not issued in series, and sometimes issued through unreliable channels of distribution.

JOURNALS

The journal has been the major dissemination medium for sciences and technologies, since the 17th cy. The first model of the modern journal, *Le Journal des Scavans* was published in France in 1665, followed by the *Philosophical Transactions* published by the Royal Society in London later in the same year. The cumulative total of scholarly articles published is estimated to have passed 50 million in 2009. (Jinha, 2010). . The Information Explosion which really took off in the post World War II phase led to a great deal of critical analysis of the role of journal and of alternatives. The major problems and possibilities were: (a)The delay between submission of a paper and its publication was too long. A delay between 7 and 16 months was reported by Campbell in 1962. (b) According to the traditional format of the journal an individual's interest is confined only in a small proportion of the papers contained in any issue. (c) Abstracting services will have to scan a wide range of journal titles to ensure adequate coverage. Further, there will be overlappings among different abstracting services, leading to a high degree of waste. (d) The incidences of rejection by editors and referees are increasing from concern about quality maintenance of the journal.

ALTERNATIVES TO JOURNALS

As an alternative to publishing in journals it is attempted at publishing Individual papers as the medium of dissemination. These individual papers will be kept in centres based on disciplines or branches of specialization and would be disseminated by branch abstracting services. Some basic drawbacks of this system were (1) some items such as letters and advertisements that may be of importance to documentation will not be reaching the users; and (2) the prestige factor of the author acceptable to an important journal is far more satisfying the interest of the author than mere inclusion in a central store.

RESEARCH REPORTS

Research reports created problems in the past because their number is too large and growing, and because they are particularly important for applied scientists and technologists. They don't even come in the purview of Invisible Colleges. Research reports emanate from mostly government departments and agencies, as classified for military/commercial security. They have to be formally declassified before they can be released. 4/5 of the world reports are produced in USA, particularly in Atomic Energy and Aerospace. But they are now systematically covered by American bibliographical services.

SECONDARY AND TERTIARY PUBLICATIONS

After the pattern of primary publication was established, scientists identified their need for two kinds of secondary services: (a) Guides to New Literature which keep them abreast of relevant advances in sciences; and (b) Guides to the Literature of the past, which help them retrieve relevant material when they need it. These were the Secondary publications which (1) lists additions to the primary literature, (2) index them for retrieval, and

(3) more often analyze the contents briefly so as to indicate or reproduce what is important.

The first abstracting journal appeared in the 18th cy. Now there are abstracting and indexing services in English for each discipline and major cross-disciplinary fields, most of them produced by learned societies or government agencies. Examples:

(a) Disciplinary

Mathematics: *Mathematical Review* (USA)

Chemistry: *Chemical Abstracts* (USA)

Physics: *Physics Abstracts* (UK)

Biology: *Biological Abstracts* (USA)

Engineering : *Computer and Control Abstracts* (USA)

(b) Cross Disciplinary

International Aerospace Abstracts (USA)

Aerospace Abstracts (USA).

Although abstracting journals are the most popular form of secondary publications they have presented serious and increasing problems to producers and users alike. These problems affect the production and use of abstracting journals.

UNDER USE OF INFORMATION

The assumption underlying the provision of secondary and tertiary services is that scientists will learn how to use them effectively and so obtain the information they need. But in actual practice we find that there is evidently under-use of these information services. The reasons for such underuse of abstracting services are several.

1. There has been a proliferation of scientific information services, but none being comprehensive. Major information systems concerned with mainly scientific literature. They excluded the technical, operational and economic information that are of

special interest to the individual industries or areas of public services.

2. They are too broad and too narrow at the same time. They are too broad in respect of locally significant research areas, and they are too narrow with respect to coverage of local subjects and publications.
3. They are abstracted in a general way for a wide variety of users and usually are not slanted to meet the special needs of special groups.
4. They lack in uniformity and standardization in respect of their classification, indexing, citation, etc,
5. They have normally comprehensive subject coverage without evaluation and selection.
6. Most of them have been disciplinary and catering for only a limited number of cross-disciplinary interests.
7. They exclude technical, operational and economic information needed by industries;
8. Abstracted in a general way and not slanted to meet the special interest groups;
9. They are included without proper evaluation and selection;
10. They being disciplinary they do not cater to cross disciplinary interest;
11. They involve undue Time Lag. Until recently, many of them have not been yielding information rapidly to users.

Solution to Time Lag lied in organizing specialized services by each organization. This led to two situations:

(a) establishment of formalized information systems and networks in each country, like Documentation centres, Referral centres, Information centres, Information Analysis centres, Computerized databases, etc,

(b) The Communication System in Science became very complex –a bewildering array of primary journals, which are covered by an equally bewildering array of secondary journals and tertiary publications.

The situation represents a haphazard growth. In order to meet one or more of the above deficiencies new specialized services have been started.

FURTHER PROBLEMS OF SPECIALIZED SERVICES

1. This led to a complex and formalized information network in each scientifically advanced country — Documentation Centres, Referral Centres, Information Centres, Information Analysis Centres, Computerized data bases, etc,
2. These scientific information systems represent a bewildering array of primary journals, which are covered by an equally bewildering array of secondary journals and tertiary journals.
3. The situation reflects a haphazard growth of scientific publications, and services among diverse organizations - professional societies, research institutes, government agencies, and commercial publishers. Further, the following features have presented more problems:
   - Services expand, contract, divide, change character in response to changes in the direction of science.
   - Frequent changes in the supply and demand for information,
   - No co-ordination between different services,
   - Much overlapping of efforts and coverage,
   - Some are in sub-disciplines,
   - Some others are on areas of application,
   - Some services are for mainly research scientists, and

— Some others are for those who apply results of science,

An individual user has to consult several of them to have a reasonable coverage. In this context, what libraries and technical information services can do?

LIBRARIES

The library is a vital part of the information chain - the very vital role in the scientific information transfer process, because (1) scientific information may be either (a) literature or (b) guides to literature. The library is vitally important for producer and consumer: (i) for those who process literature to produce secondary services, and (ii) for those who make direct use of primary and secondary literature. Hence, information centres have to be based on libraries, or supported by libraries. This situation led to development of library networks, networks of libraries of all kinds.

TECHNICAL INFORMATION CENTRES

The situation soon led to development of Technical Information Centres which have the following special features:

- They are more concerned about the contents and implications of the documents than about their bibliographical listing.
- They give more emphasis on supplying answers to specific questions either directly or by referrals to other organizations.
- They emphasize reports and patents as source materials rather than scientific journals or monographs (=newly generated information).
- They provide valuable information services to their members and also to external users (=user companies).

INVISIBLE COLLEGES

The situation also led to the formation of special groups among user groups. They are groups that communicate far more personally and regularly than others, using only informal channels. The groups comprise of the Elites of that branch of knowledge. They were named "Invisible Colleges" by De Solla Price1963). An invisible college will comprise of the most well known and respected researchers, who know one another well and communicate often.

TECHNOLOGICAL GATE KEEPERS

This is an expression made by T. J. Allen (1968). According to Allen "technological gate keepers exist in R & D laboratories. They are people to whom others run for technical discussion and consultation. They in turn maintain a greater amount of contact with professional societies, technical literature, and with technically trained friends outside the laboratory. They also attend conferences and seminars fairly frequently to keep themselves in the wave front of knowledge. They develop highly connected networks of their own. Gatekeepers exist on international level. They are in a way members of the Invisible Colleges.

SCHOLARLY COMMUNICATION IN DIGITAL FORMATS/ CHANNELS

As a result of the I T revolution several new openings for scholarly communication have been made, for both informal and formal communication hat are speedier and more instantaneous than usual.

Among them, **Electronic mail (e-mail)** is the most popular method of exchanging messages between people using electronic devices. Invented by Ray Tomlinson in 1972, e-mail by the mid-1970s had taken the form now recognized as e-mail. It is widely used for Interpersonal (person to persons) and Persons to groups (one to many) communication.

Chatting is another development. The first online chat system was called Talkomatic created by Doug Brown and David R. Woolley in 1973 at the University of Illinois. Chat refers to the processes of communicating, interacting and/or exchanging messages over the internet. It involves two or more individuals that communicate through a chat-enabled software.

Tele-conferencing (audio-visual effects) is a telephone meeting held between two or more locations through a telecommunication system. Tele-conferencing can be either voice-only or audio-video communication. Video conferencing supports the conference by providing both the video and voices of the person when others are listening to the communicator. In a teleconference either audio only or audio-video data can be transmitted via one or more different telecommunication means, such as telephone, telegraph, teletypewriter, radio, television, or computer. Particularly internet tele-conferencing includes video conferencing, web conferencing, internet telephone conferencing and Augmented Reality (AR) conferencing.

Video conferencing is the conduct of a video meeting among two or more persons who are in separate places by means of computer networks to transmit both audio and video data. Both video conferencing and teleconferencing support one –to-one or many-to-many conferences for the purpose of communication and collaboration in real time through a telecommunication system.

FORMAL COMMUNICATION

Websites and blogs

A **website** is a collection of web pages and related content that is identified by a common domain name and published on at least one web server. Only 20 years since the creation of the first website. The world wide web was born during 1991-93 by Tim Berners-Lee. He created HTML (Hypertext Markup Language). His project allowed a text-only page could be viewed using a simple line-mode browser. In 1993 was developed the Mosaic browser which later became known as the Netscape Communications. In 1996 Microsoft released its first competitive browser Flash, which was complete with its own features and HTML tags. Flash allowed the inclusion of easy animations of images, which increases interaction. Also the content became much more visual when the first version of YouTube and Flash Player could display the video content. In 1998 Netscape released the Netscape Communicator code under an open source license, enabling thousands of developers to participate in improving the software. Web design history took a serious turn toward interactive content in the late 2,000s, a phenomenon called "Web 2.0".

A **blog** (a truncation of weblog) is an online journal or informational website displaying information in the reverse chronological order, with the latest posts appearing first. It is a platform where a writer or even a group of writers share their views on an individual subject. Tumbir, Word Press, Blogger, etc. are different blogs that are popular. Blogs are different from websites. Blogs need frequent updates, whereas websites can be more static. In the early 2000s blogging emerged in all different phases when several political blogs were born. The number of bloggers in the United States is set to reach 31.7 million users in 2020. ("What is a Blog: the definition of blog, blogging and blogger", (*fistsiteguide.com*). On February 16, 2011, there were over 156 million public blogs in existence. (Blog-Wikipedia,*en.em.wikipedia.org*). Word Press, (has two iterations –Wordpress.org and Wordpress.com), Blogger, Medium, Ghost Pro, Jekyll, Viddler, Joomia, Drupal etc. are some of the different softwares or platforms used for blogging (Jennifer Young (2020).

OPEN ACCESS PUBLISHING

The enormous delay usual in getting research papers published in scientific journals made people to think of alternative measures. Open Access Publishing is one such option available. Open Access refers to freely available, digital, online information. Open access scholarly literature is free of charge and often carries less restrictive copyright and licensing barriers than traditional published works, for both the users and the authors. It is a common practice that authors are charged to bear the actual cost of publishing by the Open Access publishes, Open Access is a set of principles and a range of practices through which research outputs are distributed online, free of cost or other access barriers. Open Access publishing models allow free, immediate access to research and support the continuous, free dissemination of an author's research to an international audience of scientists, researchers, faculty and the public. Open Access publishing provides greater chances of visibility for researchers and scholars, subsequently leading to more citations and greater impact. In this system researchers can retain copyright to their intellectual property to reuse, remix or distribute their work as they wish.

PAPERS/PUBLICATIONS OVER THE NET (ORIGINALS)

In academic publishing, a paper is an academic work that is usually published in an academic journal. It contains original research results or reviews of existing results. A paper may undergo a series of reviews, revisions and re-submissions before finally being accepted or rejected for publication. The delay involved in this process is unbearable as reputed journals have longer quees awaiting publication. At present there is the option for an author/researcher to get his paper published directly on the internet without waiting for the any journal publisher to accept it for publication. The author/researcher can upload the paper directly on to the net, in appropriate websites, So also, there is the option for him to submit the paper to standard public online publishers who will present the paper for peer review. There are three possibilities after the review: It may be accepted, or accepted with revisions, or rejected. Once accepted, the manuscript is processed for uploading for online publishing.

SIMULTANEOUS DIGITAL VERSIONS OF LEARNED PERIODICALS

Some journals are 'born digital' in that they are solely published on the web in a digital format, but most electronic journals originated as print journals, which subsequently evolved to have an electronic version, while still maintaining a print component. As academic research habits have changed in line with the growth of the internet the e–journal has come to dominate the journals world. (Electronic Journal; *en.m.wiipedia.org*). However , not all print journals have an e-version, and not all e-journals are available in print.

DIGITAL LIBRARIES ONLINE

"A digital library, digital repository, or digital collection is an online database of digital objects that can include text, still images, audio, video or other digital media format" (Wikipdia). As such, "A digital library is a collection of documents on organized electronic form, available on the Internet or on CD-ROM (compact disk read-only memory) disks. Depending on the specific library, a user may be able to access magazine articles, books, papers, images, sound files and videos." (Wikipedia: *slideshare*, Digital Library). Therefore, a digital library is a library in which collections are stored in digital formats and accessible by the computers.

Some examples of digital library projects can be cited here: *World Digital Library, Universal Digital Library, Project Gutenberg, Bartleby, Ibiblio, Google Books, Internet Archive:*

The largest digital library for downloading e-books and audio –books for free, *the Open Library*: more than one million e-boos of classic literature to download. The *National Digital Library of India* contains about 48 million items. The National Science Digital Library (NSDL) was established in 2000 by the National Science Foundation (*nsdl.niscair.res.in*). The Library at the National Institute of Technology, Calicut (NITC) has established its digital library programme, called *Nalanda* – a full fledged digital library for the use of the campus community as well as for remote users from the rest of the country, particularly from southern States. Some selective digital library activities have been going on in Kerala University Library, M.G. University Library, Kerala Agricultural University Central Library, Kerala Legislature Library, Kerala State Central Library, etc. Besides, the Kerala Sahitya Akademi Library and the Appan Thampuran Library are working towards digital libraries of Malayalam books. The P.N. Panicker Foundation together with the Kerala Government I T Department have taken up the digitalization of all the public libraries in Kerala.

CONCLUSION

In scientific communication various methods and patterns were evolved in due course of time. Generally speaking, the defects/ shortcomings /disadvantages of one have led to the development of another as a step to overcome the defects /shortcomings. Thus, Scientific journals led to Research reports, Invisible colleges, information Exchange Groups, Technological Gate Keepers, to Documentation Journals : From Indexing Journals to Abstracting Journals, to Reviewing Journals, from Discipline oriented Documentation Journals to Cross- disciplinary/ Mission Oriented Journals, from Secondary Journals to Tertiary Journals, Annual Reviews, etc.

REFERENCES

ALLEN, T.J. (1968) *Aslib Proceedings* Nov.1968

Blog-Wikipedia,en.em.wikipedia.org

Electronic Journal; en.m.wiipedia.org

fistsiteguide.com.

JINHA, Arif E. "Article 50 million: an estimate of the number of scholarly articles in existence", *Learned Publishing* Vol. 23 No.4, July 2010.

MEADOWS, A.J. (1974), *Communication in Science, Butterworths.*

PRICE, De Solla, (1963) ,*Little Science Big Science*, N.Y., Columbia University Press.

Wikipedia: *slideshare*, Digital Library

YOUNG, Jennifer (2020): "16 Best: Blog Software Comparison (Free/ Open Source Tools)", *hostingadvice.com* Updated 1/27/20.

8

Barriers to Communication Process

Any System designed for human communication process may involve several problems. These problems are mainly arising out of the various elements of the communication process. The following are the elements in communication process: *Source, Message, Encoder, Medium, Channel, Decoder,* and *Destination.* The problems involved in these elements may be grouped into three:

(a) *Physical problems* – concerning the Channel, Encoder and Decoder;

(b) *Semantic problems* – concerning the Message, Medium and Meaning; and

(c) *Behavioural problems* – concerning the people involved in the process.

Every difficulty or defect in any of the elements will surely affect the communication process and will be therefore a barrier to communication process.

BARRIERS IN SCIENTIFIC COMMUNICATION

The pattern of scientific communication discussed in the previous chapter is also the basis for analyzing the barriers in communication.

INFORMAL COMMUNICATION CHANNELS

Personal letters, telephone calls, private circulation of papers and personal mailing lists are the informal channels usually adopted by scientists, The barriers in such communication are the prohibitive cost involved: (1) in postage, telephone and telefax charges both for inland communication and overseas communication. (2) E-mail communication is cheaper in the matter of recurring costs, but initial cost of computers and software and connectivity charges is involved.

PRIMARY JOURNALS

Problems for both the disseminator (transmitter) and for the receivers. A journal is a one-to-many, and many-for-one communication process. Journals are too many (numerous) to have access to the right ones. There is scattering and seepage of information in the case of primary journals: Scattering because the information on any one subject lies in different journals, and Seepage because...

SECONDARY JOURNALS

In the case of **General Documentation Services**, both Current Awareness services and Retrospective Documentation services, there are several problems for the users. *Firstly*, they are too many and selection of the appropriate one is difficult. *Secondly*, they are at the same time too broad and too narrow broad and too narrow. They are too broad when compared to the subjects, documents sought by local researchers. The topics sought after will be a very small and insignificant section of the general documentation list. At the same time the general documentation lists will be too narrow when compared to the specific subjects, documents, etc, sought after by the local researcher. *Thirdly,* they involve serious time lag. The time lag occurs in three levels: between the production of the document by the author and its submission to the documentation journal; between the date of submission and date of publication of the information in the documentation journal, and finally between the date of publication of the documentation journal and the date when the local researcher comes across the information in the documentation journal. All these put together the total delay caused will be between 2 to 3 years. *Finally,* since several documentation journals have to be surveyed by a serious researcher to get a comprehensive picture of what he seeks their differences in the classification systems used, the arrangement of data there in, and the indexes, etc, present difficulties to the user.

In the case of Local Documentation Services, the main impediments in their use are non-availability of such services in all local centres of research, and the necessity of being attached to a library having such facilities and services.

ONLINE DATABASES AND NETWORKS

The hurdles in the easy use of online databases and networks are many and varied. Firstly, the user needs to know about each data base, its special features, like scope, arrangement, etc. Secondly, the search strategy formulation involves difficulties; Thirdly, the several capital costs, like hardware, systems, software, connectivity, etc. Lastly, need for institutional support to the scientists, like membership in libraries.

INTERNET FACILITIES

Although it is common now for individuals to have direct access to Internet it involves minimum capital costs, like the availability of a desktop or laptop, connectivity (telephone network) charges, etc. Further, fuller use of the internet facilities always necessitates appropriate institutional support for the scientists.

PHYSICAL ACCESS TO DOCUMENTS

Finally, when it comes to the question of getting physical access to the documents the difficulties involved are various:

- Limited availability in the local library. The available items may not be listed in the library catalogue. Normally, library catalogues do contain information about books only. Periodicals listing will be only rarely done. Even in the case of books the catalogue does not give adequate content information.
- Limitation of the periodicals – Even when a periodical is physically accessible in the local library, the absence of cumulative indexes for that periodical necessitates intensive searching of individual volumes or issues, which is a time consuming exercise.
- Possible availability in other libraries. This entails direct contact with other libraries in the first instance, and later search for libraries which may have the document concerned. Union catalogue of books is practically nil. Union catalogues of periodicals are a possibility. Union catalogues of INSDOC and ICCSSR may help to a great extent.
- Problems with regard to Inter-library loans. In the absence of proper procedures and protocols regarding interlibrary lending and borrowing actual experience in getting materials on interlibrary loan may not be that good.
- Problems with regard to Photostat. Availability of photocopies involves payment of copying charges and postage.
- Possibility of getting Microforms. Although there is

the convenience of posting and comparatively less costly, there s the indispensability of proper equipment like the microfilm/microfiche reader, printer, etc.

- Foreign language barrier.
- Copyright regulations and restrictions.

FOREIGN LANGUAGE BARRIER

Foreign language is a significant barrier in scientific communication. The seriousness of this problem is in relation to the large volume of informational documents that fall outside the scope of the favoured language of the information user. This language scatter of informational documents arises from the following reasons:

1. Intensified research activities on a global basis;
2. Emerging nationalism and the importance of national languages;
3. International contracts and co-operation are on the increase in research and investigations;
4. Expansion of professional communities who engage in research and publications;
5. Increased online use of databases which involve more and more foreign language documents.

It is generally held that more than 50% of the world's scientific and technical literature is being published in non-English language. As English language publications dominate researchers are generally indifferent to the literature published in other languages. While it is generally held that science is universal, the channels of scientific communication cannot be considered that universal, none being multilingual and fully comprehensive.

Information users are reluctant to read materials in languages with which they are not familiar; this phenomenon has been termed "the foreign language barrier" by Rowley and Turner (1978) Foreign documents report many important advances taking place in Soviet Union and many other countries once under developed, that are in their local languages.

In 1962 about 35-50 languages continued significant amounts of scientific and technical information (Holstrom,1962). In 1966 Wood estimated the use of Earth science literature.

	NLL Collection	***Chemical Abstracts***	***Index Medicus***
English	46%	50.3%	51.2%
Russian and allied	14%	23.4%	5.6%
German	4%	3.6%	0.9%
Others	17%	9.0%	16.5%

Wood estimated that in 1967 about 750,000 articles per year were published in languages other than English.

One Unesco Study has reported about World output of science literature by Language Scatter as follows:

English = 50%

German = 20%

French = 15%

Russian = 10%

Others = 5%

OVERCOMING THE LANGUAGE BARRIER

The following measures are considered for overcoming the language barriers:

1. Common language
2. Machine translation
3. Foreign language teaching
4. Translation departments
5. External translators
6. Collections of existing translations

7. Bibliographical tools and indexes

1. Common Languages

Possibly there are two lines of approach:

(a) Accepting any one language as the universal language;

The language scatter is as English 50% and others 50%. But, English speaking people have no right to ask the other 50% of the authors to work in English. Alternatively,

(b) Development of an artificial language – All attempts in this direction have failed, like: (i) Esparanto (ii) IDO (iii) Basic English (iv) European (v) Inter-lingua.

This is simply because scientists were reluctant to learn and use artificial languages. Any artificial language unless backed by immense political and economic powers, is bound to come to the same end.

2. Machine Translation

Machine Translation is automatic translation in the sense of translation from one natural language to another by computer. This has been only partially accomplished.

Such translation can be: *letter-by-letter* (for example transliteration Morse code);*word-by-word* or *phrase -by-phrase.* Letter-by-letter translations are easier to execute, for example, production of Braille texts could be made faster and more economic by Machine Translation. Word-by-word is only a step towards phrase-by-phrase. Phrase-by-phrase translation is necessary to achieve meaningful and intelligible text translation, but it poses series of linguistic problems.

- Each language has a large vocabulary (eg, at least 40,000 words in a small English Dictionary). The computer must store and match the vocabularies of as many languages as are required.
- Homonyms where meaning is determined by context

are virtually impossible for the computer to distinguish.

- Differing word orders between languages - require that computer should scan an entire sentence and transpose words.
- Prefixes and idiomatic expressions cannot be recognized.

Because of the above linguistic problems quality translations cannot be made and the attempts at Machine Translations are almost abandoned. (For a history of attempts made in Machine Translation *see Encyclopaedia of Library & Information Science* Vol.16 Page 414-).

- Machine Translation is justified only if it is better, faster and cheaper than human translation.
- Computer cannot understand meaning of the text it is called upon to translate. The computer may translate words through the help of a bi-lingual dictionary.
- Computer cannot predict meaning. None has been able to build into a computer, knowledge of a technical field such as human specialist would have. Translation work involves not only vocabulary and grammar but also knowledge of the subject.
- Ambiguity arises when the meaning of a word or a group of words is unclear; or when they have multiple meanings they are said to be ambiguous.
- Ambiguity can exist on the word in the syntactical level (=the way of putting together, presentation and combinations), in the semantic level (=the meaning of a word in one language does not correspond exactly to the meaning of a word in the other.

There is a misunderstanding that the translator takes the word and grammar of language A , and replaces them with the words and grammar of language B. This model is not true. No translator works this way, instead, he listens to the text in language A; gets the idea, and then expresses the same meaning in language B. Meaning is the substance of communication. In order to get the idea one needs knowledge of the technical field.

3. Foreign Language Teaching/Learning

Improved language skills among information users can overcome the language barrier. One's own ability to understand own subject in foreign languages saves time and effort; without the involvement of any intermediary. At least one can decide whether to go for a full text translation or not. Scholarly knowledge of a language is often adequate for a scientist to extract pertinent details from a foreign language document. There are possible solutions in the language barrier:

1. Language teaching at school level as additional language. This is an option available in our schools. Languages like French is taught in our schools. French is being taught in Britain, and so is Russian in some other countries,.
2. Language orientation courses as part of undergraduate courses: Such courses give rudiments of a foreign language in the context of a specific discipline.
3. Postgraduate instruction in foreign language is more likely to be immediately applicable. This is also applicable for professional groups.

4. Translation Departments

Some organizations maintain internal translation services. This may be or may not be associated with the library and information service. They do this either by Employment of staff translators; or appointment of in-house translators who can interact with the inquirers and have more meaningful co-operation.

Internal translators can acquire adequate technical knowledge through such interactions with the inquirer, other employees and the library, - This cross fertilization will improve the quality and speed of the translator's work. But, no translation department can encompass all languages and subjects and that is a limitation of this option.

5. External Translators

One good option is in getting the work done by Freelance Translators, who are available in and around your home or institution. One drawback here is the product will not be so closely tailored to the needs of the organization as in the case with in-house translations. But, it may be the only available expedient in many cases. Translations are time consuming and expensive. Institutions/organization may maintain a Panel of Translators /Register of Freelance Translators. In an academic library environment there is much scope for local translators. Translation Services are rendered by important services /information /documentation centres.

Example : British Library Lending Division Translation Service (since 1957-);The BLD Programme has three components -(a)Translation of Individual periodical articles; (b)Cover to cover translation of whole journals; and (c) translation of books.

6. Collections of Existing Translations

Another option is to depend on available collections of translations . There are cover to cover translations of individual works. Besides there are adhoc translation of selected papers as are maintained, for *example*:

1. in the British Library Science Reference Library. Since 1966 National Lending Library has collected published translations in English from all languages, of science and technology monographs, individual articles, translations and cover to cover journal translations. The present BLLD by amalgamating the above two (National Science Reference Library

& NLL in 1944). There were above 275,000 individual items and complete runs of at least 250 cover to cover journals.

2. The United States National Translation Centre (NTC) in Chicago has the largest collection of Translation in United States (john Creror Library)
3. The European Translation Centre (ETC) in Delf, Netherlands, of the European Productivity Agency is another example.

PUBLICATION OF BIBLIOGRAPHICAL TOOLS AND INDEXES

Most agencies involved with the production, processing or collection of translations also compile records of translations.

Examples:

1. The *BLLD Announcement Bulletin* (supersecting the old *British Research and Development Reports* and the *NLLTranslations Bulletin*) lists report literature and other translations produced in U K by government organizations, industry, universities, learned societies and research associations.
2. The *BLLD Review* also contains select list of BLLD translations.
3. The *Commonwealth Index of Unpublished Scientific and Technical Translations* is being published by Aslib since 1951 – This was in card form housed in Australia, Canada, New Zealand and India simultaneously.
4. US National Translation Centre *Translations Register Index* from 1967-
5. Unesco Publication – *Index Translationum* is annual publication of books and monographs from all languages - Annual since 1949.
6. The European Translation Centre (ETC) is publishing

the *World Index of Scientific Translations* (a monthly with quarterly and annual cumulations) – *Translation Journals* is an annual supplement to the *World Index*.

LANGUAGE SITUATION IN INDIA

Indian scientists have, due to historical reasons, preference for English language. Foreign languages, other than English, did not play any role in the scientific development of India during the pre-independent period. After independence the situation changed :

(a) There arose multilateral collaboration with countries having different languages;

(b) There was, among the student communities, an Increasing interest in the study of foreign languages - for purposes of study abroad or for seeking employments abroad.

(c) Most of the important foreign languages have begun to be teaching in Indian universities.

(d) In some universities/research institutions knowledge of at least one foreign language is prescribed compulsory for M. Phil/Ph.D. admissions.

(e) Finally, English is being maintained as the medium of instruction for higher education, English continued to be the language of science in India.

(f) Indian scientists cite have a preference for citing more of English documents (69.6% in a study conducted in 1972).

(g) Russian was the most popular foreign language in India next to English – due to various political, economic, scientific and technical, and cultural links India had with USSR.

At present Indian scientists have to face two language problems:

(a) Information is published in Regional Languages in which they are not proficient; and

(b) Information is published in foreign languages among which English is the only language in which they are proficient.

TRANSLATION SERVICES IN INDIA

In India, the activities of NISCAIR (formerly INSDOC) deserves special mention: They are

(a) Responsive translation : NISCAIR has been providing translation service from many foreign languages into English and also vice versa, to the scientists since the inception of INSDOC in 1952. Such translations on specific requests is carried out by either in-house translators or party-time translators chosen from the Roster of Translators the organization maintains. The translation service is made available to govt. departments, universities, R&D organizations, public sector undertakings, industries, etc.

(b) Translation for National Science Foundation (USA) : Under an agreement with US National Science Foundation, INSDOC had undertaken since 1967 a cover to cover translation of foreign language documents assigned by them. NSF has been giving funds for this project.

(c) Russian Science Information Centre &Digest Service : On the basis of a bilateral agreement signed with the Soviet Union in 1970 INSDOC established in 1971 the Russian Science Information Centre. The objective was to make available to Indian scientists currently published materials in USSR. INSDOC receives under this programme about 3000 publications and 350 current titles of Soviet periodicals every year. The lists of both the items are brought out and distributed by INSDOC.

(d) National Index of Translations : INSDOC has been publishing a monthly periodical reporting in a classified sequence translations of S & T literature in foreign languages done by about 21 R & D institutions in India.

TRANSLATION PROCESSES

Translation processes can be grouped into:

1. Literal translation - word-by-word for factual type materials;
2. Non-literary translation – free translation –only for literary works like poetry based on ideas or emotions, attitudes and literary styles of original;
3. Responsive translation - done on specific demandAnticipatory translation – For example are: cover to cover translation of journals; translation of selected papers from different periodicals;
4. Literary translation – style and technique of expressing feelings are significant;
5. Scientific translation – precision is more relevant.

TRANSLATION PERSONNEL

With regard to translation personnel there can be:

Translation by specialists, or

Translation by professionals.

In either case, the Qualities Required of Translators of scientific materials (in the order of importance) are:

1. Knowledge of the technical field of the text;
2. Native command of the language to be translated into;
3. Knowledge of the language to be translated from.

ARTIFICIAL LANGUAGES

Mention was already made about the development of artificial languages in order to meet the foreign language barrier. Some of the main attempts in this direction are discussed below:

1. Esperanto : This was invented by Louis Zamenlooff, a German Physician, in the late 19th cy. It claims to have 15 million speakers all over the world. Its appeal is mainly to those having Western European languages as mother tongues; because Esperanto's grammatical structure, forms and roots are based on those common to English, French, German, Italian and Spanish. In effect, it is another foreign language to others.

2. IDO is another artificial language developed from Esperanto. However, this has only less significance than Esperanto.

3. Basic English : This is the simplified English with a vocabulary of 800 words, and it was introduced since World War Ii.

4. European : In 1979 there was another proposal to introduce *European* – as a mixture of all European languages.

5. Inter-lingua : This is based on the simplification of Latin. But it is in favour of one family of languages only.

COPYRIGHT BARRIER

WHAT IS COPYRIGHT?

Copyright restricts the copying of the physical material that embodies any literary or artistic work. Unlike other controls relating to intellectual property (e.g. patents, trademarks and registered designs) copyright protects the form of the words or the actual physical expression and **not the ideas** represented in a document. Copyright is intended to define the author's or artist's interests in that the author and his publisher receives sufficient remuneration to encourage them to continue writing and publishing. It is assumed that the copyright is infringed by the unauthorized production of enough copies to affect adversely the sale of the original.

The **Question addressed here is:** To what extent copyright restrictions affect the dissemination of information?

HISTORY OF COPYRIGHT

In England until the arrival of printing the author's rights were acknowledged. But with printing, the printer wanted some legislative protection against unfair competition – So, king began to give printer's licenses.

In 1556 the Star Chamber Decree was issued by which the Stationery Company was to control printing and dissemination of printed matter in the interests of Church and State. All printers were obliged to take membership in the Stationer's Company and to register all books having copyright. The Common Law gave the legal protection.

In 1643, Act for Redressing Disorders in Printing was passed- This made it compulsory to obtain an author's permission before reproducing his work.

In 1709, Copyright Act of Queen Anne was the earliest legislation to vest copyright in the author. Registration was later made compulsory in Stationer's Company. According to this Act, copyright was protected for 21 years in the case of already printed works and for 14 years for books not printed then.

In 1911 Copyright Act discarded compulsory registration with Stationer's Company as a condition for bringing infringement action.

In 1956 the Copyright Act protected the copyright covering literary, dramatic, and musical works, works of art (drawings, etc.), films, sound recordings, television and sound broadcasts.

The fundamental concept of copyright as laid down in the Act was:

"The exclusive right to copy and to authorize other people to copy, is automatic, in the context of an "original work" written by a "qualified person". The owner of the copyright is the author. The Act forbids:

(a) Reproducing the work

(b) Publishing the work

(c) Making an adaptation of the work

(d) Publishing or reproducing any adaptation of the work.

EXEMPTIONS FROM COPYRIGHT

There are some exemptions from Copyright. Copying does not constitute infringement if it is "fair dealing" for the purpose of:-

1. Research or private study - Normally not taken as "unfair" if a single copy is made.
2. Criticism or Review – Up to 1/5 of the complete book can be quoted.
3. Reporting current events in a newspaper or magazine or for broadcasting.
4. Judicial Proceedings.
5. Short passages in collections for use in schools.

EXEMPTIONS FOR LIBRARIES AND ARCHIVES

1. No infringement of copyright of an article in a periodical by making or supplying a copy of the article provided:
   (a) the library is not established or conducted for profit,
   (b) the librarian is convinced that the copy is required for research or private study.
   (c) No person may be given two or more copies of the same article.
   (d) No copy extends to more than one article in any one publication.
2. The copying of extracts from books provided the extract copying is not a reasonable proportion of the book.
3. Copying of a **whole work** is permitted exclusively by one librarian for a librarian at another non-profit

making library.

4. Photocopying/other reprography services are not prevented by Copyright Regulations therefore not a barrier in communication.

(5) Printing of local editions not possible because of copyright protection of foreign publications. Therefore users/libraries are compelled to buy the foreign publications at the prohibitive prices.

International Copyright

There are two main international copyright conventions:

- The Berne Copyright Convention 1886
- the Universal Copyright Convention 1954

Countries belonging to Berne Convention undertake to grant reciprocal protection to one another's works – **period is life plus 50 years.** Berne Convention is not binding on the United States. US has bilateral copyright agreements.

Universal Copyright Convention, 1954 was sponsored by Unesco. It presents that copies of a work are to be endorsed by ©, the year of publication and the name of the copyright owner.

Some countries do not belong to any copyright union, like Soviet Union and China.

REFERENCES

CHAKRABORTY, A.R., et. al. "Translations and Translation Services" *Annals of Library and Information Studies* Vol 22 (2) June 1975; P.60-72, *Encyclopaedia of Library & Information Science* Vol.16 Page 414-

FISHMAN, Stephen (2008): *The Copyright Handbook: What Every Writer Needs to Know,* Edn .10, Nolo, 2008; 527 p.

HOLSTROM, J.E. 1962), *Aslib Proceedings* December 1962.

ROWLEY, J.E. and TURNER, G M D (1978), *The dissemination of information,* Boulder Co., Western Press, p. 298.

STRONG, William (1981): *The Copyright book*, MIT Press.

TANEJA, S.K. (1979), "Translation Services; Their Organisation and Documentation at National Level in India", *Annals of Library and Information Studies* Vol 26 (1-4): March –December, 1979.

WOOD, D.N. Ed. (1966), *Use of Earth Sciences literature,* Butterworth, London, 1966.

9

Bibliometrics

Bibliometrics is the quantitative treatment of properties of recorded information. "Bibliometrics is that branch of information theory that attempts to analyze quantitatively the properties and behaviour of recorded knowledge (Prichard,1969). Bibliometry is of recent origin, relatively new. It has emerged as a significant research area. 1/9 of all the articles published in Library and Information Science area are on bibliometrics and related topics. Now bibliometric techniques are used in various disciplines in Social Sciences and Sciences to study the **theory of literature structure.**

GENESIS AND DEVELOPMENT

Firsts appeared as Statistical Analysis by Cole and Eale (1917), and in 1923 Hulme called it "Statistical Bibliography". Since then the name was used by many. It was in 1969 that A. Pritchard suggested the word "Bibliometrics" as the name "Statistical Bibliography" was found very clumsy and can be confused with Statistics itself or bibliographies on Statistics. Prichard (1969) defined "bibliometrics" as *"The application of mathematical methods to books and other media of communication"*.

There were also other names proposed and used in literature, namely **Librametics, Scientometrics** and **Informetrics**. Bibliometrics is analogous with Dr. Ranganathan's "Librametrics". "Scientometrics" is the Russian concept while "Informetrics" is the name introduced by FID.

One of the classical definitions of bibliometrics is the one given by Raising in 1962: "*The assembling and interpretation of statistics relating to books and periodicals...to demonstrate historical movements, to determine national and universal research, use of books and journals and to ascertain in many local situations the general use of books and journals*".

According to R. A. Fairthorne (1969), it is "*the quantitative treatment of properties of recorded discourses and behaviour appertaining to it*". W.G. Potter (1983), defined bibliometrics as "*the study and measurement of the publication patterns by all forms of written communication and their authorship*". The term "Scientometrics" used often in the same sense as "bibliometrics" had its origin in Russia to mean, "*the application of quantitative methods to the history of science*".

BIBLIOMETRIC LAWS

Bibliometric laws are empirically founded statistical regularities. They are not natural laws but only behavioural patterns of users and authors. They are useful in designing a system to function effectively and in turn may modify the behaviour of users and authors so that the laws may even cease to apply. In other words, the feedback mechanism may lead to changes in the original distribution.

The three laws that have gained recognition as **bibliometric laws** are given below:

1. Lotka's Law (about the productivity of authors),
2. Zipf's Law (about the frequency of occurrence of words in a text),

3. Bradford's Law (of scattering of journal literature).

LOTKA'S LAW (INVERSE SQUARE LAW)

In 1926 Alfred J. Lotka brought out a measure of the productivity of authors within the subject Chemistry. For this the *decennial index* of *Chemical Abstracts1907-16* and counted the names against which 1, 2, 3, etc appeared. He tabulated data for 6891 names under only letter 'A' and 'B'. Lotka was a statistician in an insurance company. According to him if one knows the number of authors writing one paper each only, one can predict the number of authors writing two, three or more. In Chemistry the factor was 1/n2 where 'n' is the number of papers per author. The number of persons making 2 contributions is about one-fourth of those making one contribution, the number making 'n' contributions is about 1/n2 of those making one. It would be like this: For every 100 authors contributing one article, 25 will contribute 2 articles, about 11 will contribute 3 articles and 6 will contribute 4 articles and so on.

Lotka's Law on the Productivity of Authors

Authors	Papers
100	1 each
25	2 each
11	3 each
6	4 each
4	5 each

This particular distribution seems to emerge with an amazing regularity when applied to the fields of hard sciences.

Lotka's Law has led to many studies on scientific productivity. This has led to the new discipline called "Scientometrics", which can be defined as the study of the measurement of scientific and technological progress. Many things could be studied:

- the structure of scientific activity;
- the disciplines being researched;
- the organizations involved;
- the strength and deficiency in the scientific groups and then communication channels.
- It enables econometric studies through the use of quantitative data, concepts and models and extensive use of mathematical and statistical techniques of modeling and data analysis.
- Study of the impact of social change on scientific productivity;
- Relationship of publication output as scientific recognition;
- Identification of elites in different disciplines;
- Occurrence of discoveries in different cultures, etc, etc,

An interesting study of scientific productivity made in 1962 by M. Yuasa about the scientific achievements in various countries showed that the world scientific dominance was shifting from country to country - from Italy to Britain, from Britain to France, from France to Germany and finally to USA in the 20th century.

ZIPF'S LAW OF WORD OCCURRENCE

Zipf developed in 1949 an extended empirical law, governing a relation between the rank of a word and the frequency of its appearance in the long text. His law states that in a long textual matter if words are arranged in their decreasing order of frequency, then the rank of any given word of the text will be inversely proportional to the frequency of occurrence of the word.

Zipf's Law can be used in the generation of semi-automatic or automatic indexes useful

- for an information retrieval system, especially in natural language indexing of textual matter in electronic form.
- to find out the pattern of frequency distribution of descriptors of a thesaurus and the distribution of indexing terms;
- to assess the richness in the vocabulary of an author, for using in the detection of authorship in disputed cases – by finding out the frequency of occurrence of favourite words; and
- to identify the words more frequently used in foreign languages.

Zipf's Law was originally formulated in terms of quantitative linguistics, stating that given some corpus of natural language utterances, the frequency of any word is inversely proportional to its rank in the frequency table. Thus the most frequent word will occur approximately twice as often as the second most frequent word, three times as often as third most frequent word, etc: the rank frequency distribution is an inverse relation. For example, in the *Brown Corpus* of American English text, the word "*the*" is the most frequently occurring word, and by itself accounts for nearly 7% of all word occurrences (69,971 out of slightly over 1 million). True to Zipf's Law, the second-place word "*of*" accounts for slightly over 3.5% of words (36,411 occurrences), followed by "*and*" (28,852). Only 135 vocabulary items are needed to account for half the *Brown Corpus.*

The Law is named after the American linguist George Kingsley Zipf (1902-1950), who popularized it and sought to explain it though he did not claim to have originated it.

BRADFORD'S LAW OF SCATTERING

Bradford's Law is one of the most fruitful for Information workers. S.C. Bradford was the Keeper of Science Museum in London. The Law was formulation

1948. It states that if a group of journals are arranged in an order of decreasing productivity, that is, the journal that yields the most relevant articles coming first and the most unproductive last, then the journals will be grouped into a number of zones each producing a similar number of relevant articles. However, the number of journals in each zone will be increasing very rapidly.

Zone	Number of Journal titles	Number of papers
1	9	429
2	59	499
3	258	404

The relationship he represented as 1:a: a2 when 'a' is about 5. That is the second zone has five times the number of journals of the first zone, and the third zone 52 or 10/25 times the number of journals is the first or nucleus zone.

S.C. Bradford in 1934 published a paper showing the dispersion/scattering amongst scientific periodicals of articles about 'applied geophysics' and about 'lubrication'. The paper was reprinted in 1948 with minor alterations. In both these largely unrelated topics he grouped the source periodicals into three zones in order of decreasing yield, each zone yielding the same number of required articles. Bradford found the number of periodicals in each zone to increase geometrically. He used this finding to estimate the number of periodicals that contained articles on a specific subject and concluded that, unless many pertinent articles were to be lost, periodical literature must be abstracted by source and not by subject.

Bradford's Law was formulated only in 1948. The Law states that "if a group of journals are arranged in an order of decreasing productivity on a specific topic (that is the journal that yields the most relevant articles coming first, and the most unproductive last) then the journals will be grouped into a number of zones each producing a similar number of relevant articles, the number of journals in each zone will be increasing very rapidly".

This relationship be represented as 1:a:a2 where 'a' is about 5. This means that the second zone has five times the number of journals of the first zone, and the third zone 52 or 25 times the number of journals in the first (nucleus) zone. Applications of Bradford's Law are in (1) collection building and (2) in deciding the scope of coverage of indexing work.

Bradford's Law was further extended by many notably including B.C. Vickery in 1948, Kendall in 1960, Leimkuhler in1967, and Brooks in 1969. Of these Kendall worked on Bradford-Zipf equivalence.

Reasons for Bradford's Distribution

1. Editors of journals want to publish articles from as many different authors as possible.
2. The authors want to restrict themselves to core journals.
3. Core journals reject many articles.

OTHER WORKS IN BIBLIOMETRICS

The three empiric laws that became the cornerstones of bibliometrics are;

1. Lotka's inverse square law about the productivity of authors,
2. Zipf's law about the frequency of occurrence of words in a text; and
3. Bradford's law of scattering of articles.

Several researchers gave attempted to bring out the inter-relationship among the three major bibliometric laws of Lotka, Zipf and Bradford. Also much of the later studies were made either to substantiate, modify, extend, link or challenge these three empiric laws. These studies have also led to the emergence of more empirical laws and many theoretical models. A systematic study of these laws was done by Robert A. Fairthorne in the year 1969.

Some of the other empirical laws are:

1. Price's Square Root Law of Scientific Productivity

This law states that "half of the scientific papers are contributed by the square root of the total number of scientific authors".

2. Garfield's Law of Concentration

Relatively few journals are involved in the publishing of an overwhelming majority of the material in a subject. A study of the *Science Citation Index* (SCI) database showed that 500 journals accounted for 70% of the material indexed in SCi in 1969. About half of the 3.85 million references published in that year was found to emanate from only 250 journals. This evidence is drawing away from Bradford's Law of Scattering to Garfield's Law of Concentration. The Law states that "*a basic concentration of journals is the common core or nucleus of all fields*". There is a large overlap among disciplines that the core literature of all scientific disciplines involves a group of not more than 1000 journals.

3. Sen Gupta's Law of Bibliometrics

This is basically an extension of the Bradford's Law. It states that: "*during phases of rapid growth of knowledge in a scientific discipline, articles of interest to that discipline appear in increasing number of periodicals distant from that field*".

AGEING AND OBSOLESCENCE OF PUBLICATIONS

It is commonly believed that recently published / emitted information/messages are more likely to be demanded by recipients than older messages. For example:

Out of date time tables are of no use to the traveller;

Last month's share prices are not interesting to the stockbroker (unless...)

Publishers let many books go out of print because demand for them falls off. The volume of use is related to the age of the items sought.

Many studies have been made of obsolescence of publications . One of the earliest reported was by C.C. Barnard, in 1938 As the title of the paper makes it evident Barnard's study was of the use of periodicals in a medical library, over a period 5 years (1931-35). The data brought out by him was as follows:

Number of items with years of publication

1931- 1935	2863
1926-1930	3278*
1921-1925	1643
1916-1920	866
1911-1915	737
1906-1910	495
1896-1900	174
1891-1895	84
1886-1890	62
1886-1935	10,202

The use of items published during 1926-30 (=3278) is about 53 times higher than those in 1886-1890 (=62). That is 3278 divided by 62 is equal to 52.87.

M.B. Line (1970) pointed out that the part of the lower use of older material was simply due to the fact there was less older material available to be used

It is often found that most studies of obsolescence do not take this fact into account – a point established by Line and Sanderson (1974) against the hypotheses of obsolescence.

Most investigators would maintain that, by and large, the relative use of an item of information declines as it grows older. That is, the relative use of an item of information declines as it grows older.

Griffith and others in 1979 did a careful experimental study by examining citations as an indicator of the use of scientific articles. One of their findings was that it is during the first 25 years that obsolescence occur.

REFERENCES

BARNARD, C.C. (1938) "The selection of periodicals for medical and scientific libraries", *Library Association Record*, 40:549-57.

BRADFORD, S.C. (1934) "Sources of information on specific subjects", *Engineering* 137:85-86.

BRADFORD, S.C. (1948), *Documentation*, Crosby Lockwood and sons, London.

BROOKS, B.C. (1969) "Bradford's Law and the Bibliography of Science", *Nature* 224:953-956.

BROOKS, B.C. (1979) "The Bradford's Law: a new calculus for the social sciences?" *Journal of American Society for Information Science*, 30(4):233-54.

COLE, E.J. and EALE, N.B.J. (1917), *The history of comparative Anatomy, Part I : A statistical analysis of literature. Science Progress*11: April 1917.

FAIRTHORNE, R. A.(1969), "Empirical Hyperbolic distribution (Bradford-Zipf Model lost) for bibliometric descrlption and prediction" *Journal of Documentation* 25:1969, p..319].

FAIRTHORNE, Robert A. (2005), "Empirical hyperbolic distributions for bibliometric distribution and prediction" *in Journal of Documentation* Vol. 61(2), January 2005, Pp.171-193.

GARFIELD, Eugene (1971) "The mystery of the transposed journal lists; wherein Bradford's Law of Scattering is generalized according Garfield's law of concentration", *Current Contents* 31 (1971):5-6

GOFFMAN, W. and Warren, K.S. (1969) "Dispersion of papers among journals based on a mathematical analysis of two diverse medical literatures" *Nature* 221: 1205-1207.

GOFFMAN, W. and WARREN, K.S. (1980): *Scientific Information Systems and Principle of selectivity*, New York, Praeger .

GRIFFITH, et.al. (1979), "Ageing of scientific literature: a citation analysis" *Journal of Documentation* 35(179-196).

GUPTA, Sen I.N. (1973) "Recent growth of the literature of Biochemistry and changes in ranking of periodicals" *Journal of Documentation* 29 (2): 210-211.

HULME, E. Wyndham (1923), *Statistical Bibliography in relation to the growth of Modern civilization*, London, Butler & Turner Grafton.

KESSLER, M.M. (1963) "Bibliographic Coupling Between Scientific Papers", *American Documentation*, 14(1963):10-25.

LEIMKUHLER, F.F.(1967) "The Bradford Distribution", *Journal of Documentation*, 23(3) Pp.197-207.

LINE, M. B. (1970) "The half –life of periodical literature; apparent and real obsolescence", *Journal of Documentation* 26 (46-54).

LINE, M.B. and Sanderson, A. (1974), "Obsolescence and changes in the use of literature with time" *Journal of Documentation* 30:283-350.

LOTKA, Alfred J. (1926)"The frequency of distribution of scientific productivity" *Journal of the Washington Academy of Sciences* 16(12), 19 June1926 pp.317-323.

POTTEER, W.G. (1981), "Introduction to Bibliometrics" *in Library Trends* 30:1981

PRICE, Derek J. de Solla (1965) "Networks of Scientific Papers"...

PRITCHARD, Alan (1969) "Statistical bibliography or bibliometrics?" *Journal of Documentation* 20(4) December 1969.

RAISING, L. Miks. (1962), "Statistical bibliography in health sciences" *Bull of the Medical Library Association* 50:1962; pp.450-461.

RANGANATHAN, S.R. (1948) "Librametry"; concept presented at the ASLIB Conference held at Lemington Spa.

VICKERY, B.C. (1948) "Bradford's Law of scattering, *Journal of Documentation* 4 (3), PP.198-203.(1948).

*Wikipedia. Zipf's Law en.m.wikipedia.*org down loaded on 08 April 2020

YUASA ,M. (1962), "Centre of Scientific Activity: its shift from the

16th to the 20th Century", *Japanese Studies in the History of Science*, No.1, 1962 Pp. 57-75.

Zipf, George Kingsley (1935). *The Psychobiology of Language*, Houghton-Mifflin.

Zipf, George Kingsley (1949). *Human behavior and the Principles of Least Effort*, Cambridge Massachusetts, Addison Wesley.

10
Sociology of Information

WHAT IS SOCIOLOGY?

Sociology is the science of the society, dealing with the social structures, systems, institutions, practices and values, the forces governing the people who live in groups, and all issues connected with group living. Most frequently, sociology is simply defined as the science of society, society referring to a group of people who share a common inter dependent life through inter action and inter relationships. We might say that sociology is a particular (scientific) means of making discoveries and explanations regarding human social behaviour.

To understand what sociology is, we must see it in three different dimensions: *First*, we must have a general idea of the subject matter that sociologists are concerned with. *Second*, we must be aware of the methods prescribed for the study of the subject matter. *Third*, is the conceptual frame of reference for the analysis of human social behaviour which the sociologist brings to his subject matter.

The objectives of sociology, according to Kinch (1971) are to discover and explain the nature of social behaviour, applying the rules of science, the method restricting the sociologist to those data that are revealed through observation and experience – i.e. empirical data.

Sociology is the science that deals with social groups, their internal forms or modes of organization, the processes that tend to maintain or change those forms of organization and the relations between groups.

Sociology includes study of institutionalization, structure of social systems, culture, socialization, marriage and family, kinship systems, religion and religious groups and subsystems, stratification –social classes, social deviation and social change, ideology, etc. and even the economy as a subsystem of society, economic institutions, the polity and political democracy.

Sociology, for many, provides a theoretical foundation for applied sciences, According to Auguste Comte (1853), sociology as a positive science could establish laws of social behavior.

SOCIOLOGY OF INFORMATION

Sociology is concerned with the study of human social behaviour. Information is basically a social phenomenon. The study of information science is directly concerned with the study of information, how they are generated, transferred (communicated) and used. All these involve problems of human behavior. Hence sociology of information is the study of the social aspects of information generation, communication and utilization.

Sociology of Information is a subject area dealing with all the social issues connected with information. The very foundation of this subject area is that information is a social phenomenon.

One significant area in sociology of information is communication behaviour in respect of the producers, distributors, and end users of information.

USER STUDIES

Significance and Relevance

The three major concerns of Information Science are:

- Study of Information;
- Study of Communication process; and
- Study of Information Systems.

When you study information as a phenomenon the properties and behaviour of information are also studied. When you study the Communication Process the communication patterns are also studied. And when you study the Communication Patterns there are two approaches possible: (a) Study of the behavior of literature; and (b)Study of the behaviour of users.

User Studies may be concerned with:

- either studying the information processing activities of users;
- or empirical studies of the use of, or demand or need for, information.

PURPOSE OF USER STUDIES

User Studies are intended:

= generally to further the understanding of the processes involved in information transfer;

= they may lead to the improvement of information transfer systems of all types; and

= they may lead to the general improvement of services,

GENESIS AND DEVELOPMENT

User Studies have their genesis in the 1930s when Louis R. Wilson studied the status of libraries in the United States. From 1948 to 1958 the Royal Society of Information Conferences held in London and Washington respectively. During this period, J.D. Bernal in 1948, Ralph R. Shaw in 1956 brought out their significant studies. Bernal studied the use of scientific information based on questionnaire method. Shaw studied the use of scientific literature based on questionnaire and diary. Since then, large amount of user studies has come out. A turning point in the history of user studies was the establishment of CRUS (The Centre for Research on User Studies) by the British Library Research & Development Division, at the University of Sheffield in 1975.

NEED FOR USER STUDIES

User Studies was found necessary for a systematic approach in evaluating and organizing library and information services. The objectives of such studies may include:

1. Judging the efficiency of Library and Information Service systems;
2. Identifying the levels and trends of user needs;
3. Innovating more cost-effective methods of library researches;
4. Enhancing the quality of the collection through changing the collection development programmes;
5. Identifying the problems that reduce or prevent the fuller use of the library and its resources and to find appropriate solutions:
6. Identifying the future information needs and demands; and
7. Designing and developing need-based /user oriented information systems.

THREE SUB-AREAS OF USER STUDY

According to Prof. Herbert Menzel (1966) user studies fall into three categories: (a) Behaviour studies, (b) Use studies, (3) Information flaw studies. Studies that deal with the pattern of overall information of the user's community with the communication system without reference to any specific information receiving event – are called communication behavior studies. Studies conducted to find out the use of any communication medium such as primary journals, secondary journals, etc, are called Use Studies. Studies that are conducted to find out the pattern of flow of information in the communication system are called information flow studies.

WHO CONSTITUTE THE USER COMMUNITY?

Users are broadly speaking, those who are at least using the library and its service once in a year. Users can be divided by age, by sex, by occupation, by subject specialization, etc. Information users can also be grouped as:

1. Potential users (those who need),
2. Expected users (those intending to use),
3. Actual users (those used), and
4. Beneficiary users (those benefitted) .

WHAT ALL THINGS CAN BE STUDIED?

- The range of information sources they use;
- The relative usefulness of the different sources;
- The background, motivation, professional orientation, and other individual characteristics of users;
- The social, political, economic and psychological factors affecting users;
- The consequences of information use – the results; and Anything else.

HOW TO STUDY THE USERS?

Information use is a behaviour and data are collected on any behavior

1. by asking people about it,
2. by observing the occurrences, and

3. by examining its artifacts (e.g. documents/ proofs)

The methodologies now used are diverse and as are applicable to the special problems/phenomena studied.

CONVENTIONAL METHODS

The convention methods used in User Studies are generally fourfold as is used in social surveys. They are:

1. Questionnaire,
2. Interview,
3. Diary, and
4. Observation by self.

Questionnaires may be structured or unstructured. Questions framed to ascertain the user needs, use pattern and use behaviour. These are in the case of structured questionnaire.

Unstructured questionnaire are used for Interviews. There are two types of interviews also – structured and unstructured. Structured interviews are conducted by using a pre-designed questionnaire.

There can be difference between typical and habitual information use.

THE DIARY STUDY

It has been there since 1948 (Bernal). The Diary recordings reflect the typical behavior of information users. It may lead to information on a series of critical incidents if the diary relates to an on-going task. There are of course some drawbacks for the Diary Study. It depends on the earnestness in maintaining a Diary as the true record of happenings in the information episode of the user. It is likely that a Diary is filled with details recollected haphazard after the information episode is over.

OBSERVATION

Observation as the name implies, is a way of collecting data through observing. Observation consists of receiving knowledge of the outside world through our senses, or recording information using scientific tools and instruments. Any data recorded during an experiment can be called an observation. Observation as a data collection method can be structured or unstructured. Structured or systematic observation, data collection is conducted during specific variables and according to pre-defined schedule. Unstructured observation, on the other hand, is conducted in an open and free manner in a sense that there would be no pre-determined variables or objectives. The disadvantage of observation is the high levels of observer bias, and impact of observer on primary data, in a way that presence of observer may influence the behaviour of sample group of elements.

NON-CONVENTIONAL METHODS

There are many special methods found applicable in User Studies. They are:

- Critical Incident Method
- The Solution Development Record,
- The Participant Observer Technique,
- The Sociometric Analysis,
- Citation Analysis or Document Analysis,
- Experiments and Quasi Experiments in Field Settings,
- Psychometric Method,
- Cognitive Organization,
- Computer –based Research, and
- Solution Development Method

Critical Incident Method

There are critical incident information use and Information chunk concept. The information chunk is the smallest quantity of information required to answer a task-related question.

A critical Incident is any actual or alleged event or situation that creates a significant risk of substantial or serious harm to the physical or mental health, safety or well being of a waiver participant. The Critical Incident Technique is a research method in which the research participant is asked to recall and describe a time when a behaviour, action, or occurrence impacted (either positively or negatively) a specified outcome (for example, the accomplishment of a given task).

Solution Development Record

In this method, diary entering scientist's estimate of the likely solutions to the problems he is working on is used for data analysis. T.J. Allen (1965) surveyed information sources and their effectiveness in parallel research and development programmes for laboratory facilities. He examined three pairs of parallel R & D projects. The data analyzed were gathered by means of Solution Development Records – a form which provides a weekly estimate of probability of adoption of the approaches under consideration as possible solutions to a technical problem.

Participant Observer Technique

Participant observation is one type of data collection method by practitioner-scholars typically used in qualitative research and ethnography. Ethnographic details include details of people in their cultural setting. The technique was originally used by Bronislaw Malinoiwski in 1929. Since then It was used extensively by many including Frank Hamilton Cushing (1990) in his study of the Zuni people in the latter half of the 19th century. This type of methodology is employed in many disciplines, particularly anthropology, sociology, communication studies, human geography and social psychology. In this method the behaviour of each scientist will be observed by a participant observer, working as an information assistant for each scientist. He will be trained in record keeping. There are four types of observational research ranging from detached observation with no participation on your part, namely Complete Observer, Observer as Participant, Participant as Observer, and Complete Participant. The strength of Participant Observation is the depth of knowledge that it allows the researcher to obtain and the perspective of knowledge of social problems and phenomena generated from the level of the everyday lives of those experiencing them.

Sociometric Analysis

Sociometric Analysis is an analysis technique which has a group and not an individual chosen as it unit for the analysis. It has this name as its foundation lies in Sociology. Sociometry incorporates the measurement of choice, communication and interpersonal relationship of the people belonging to different groups. Sociometry is a quantitative method for measuring social relationships and is based on the fact that people make choices in interpersonal relationships. For example, society refers to applying of interpersonal likes and preferences within a classroom. Historically the term sociometrics is associated with the work of J. L. Moreno (1934). Now this is a well developed research methodology, and is concerned with the study of the influence of interpersonal relations among scientists, in both Informal and formal communications. This research method is very widely used in studying group relations especially in the educational context (Jennings, H.H. 1987) and Smith and Vickers There is also the development of the discipline of Computerized Sociometry (Treadwell, et. al. 1998).

Citation Analysis/Document Analysis

Citation studies are the evidences of the use made of documentary sources of information. This as a research method has been widely used in Library and Information

Science. Plotting networks of papers. Identifying reciprocal citations, etc. are done in such studies. In citation studies what are studied are connections among documents rather than people.

Citation analysis is s way of measuring the relative importance or impact of an author, an article or a publication by counting the number of times that author, article, or publication has been cited by other works. Citation Analysis is the examination of the frequency, patterns, and graphs of citations in documents. It used the directed graph of citations to reveal links from one document to another document and to reveal various properties of the documents. A typical task would be to identify the most important documents in a collection. A classic example, is that of the citations between academic articles and published books. Another example is: judges of law support their judgments by referring back to judgments made in earlier cases. Similar example is provided by patents which contain prior art, citation of earlier patents relevant to the current claim. The citations in a collection of documents can also be represented in forms such as a fitting graph as pointed out by Derek J. de Solla Price in his 1965 article "Networks of Scientific Papers" Citation analysis tools can be used to compute various impact measures for scholars based on data from citation indices.

Eugene Garfield developed this into Science Citation Index. In 1955 Garfield published his ground breaking paper on citation indexing "Citation Indexes for Science: A New Dimension in Documentation through Association of ideas". This innovative paper envisioned information tools that allow researchers to expedite their research process, evaluate the impact of their work, spot scientific trends, and trace the history of modern scientific thoughts. Three years later in 1958, In 1960, Garfield laid the foundations for ISI (Institute for Scientific Information) in Philadelphia. Later in 1964, he proposed the publication of *Science Citation Index* and he brought out a five volume print edition indexing 613 journals and 1.4 million citations which two years later became available on magnetic tape. These were later made available in a Web environment to give birth to the *Web of Science*. Garfield's vision was ahead of its time. He saw the potential of citation searching for researcher, but it took 40 years for the technology to advance to the point that allowed his vision to be fully realized (Yancey, R. 2005). More than one million citations from the scientific literature have been processed by the Science Citation Index Project at the Institute of Scientific Information, Philadelphia. The project was sponsored by National Science Foundation (NSF) and National Institute of Health (NIH).

Experiments and Quasi Experiments in Field Settings

Beyond passive observation, experiments can be designed and studied.. An experiment is an investigation in which a hypothesis is scientifically tested. Field Experiments are studies using experimental design that occur in a natural setting. Instead of a laboratory setting, the experiments are carried out in the field, or the real world. Experiments conducted in a laboratory setting use the laboratory as an environment because researchers have more control over how they manipulate or influence independent variables. A quasi-experiment is an empirical interventional study used to estimate the casual impact of an intervention on target population without random assignment. In a true experiment research participants have an equal chance of being assigned to a condition of the independent variable (the one being manipulated by the researcher) that is involved in the study. Quasi-experiments are employed when the researcher is interested in independent variables that cannot be randomly assigned.

Beyond passive observation experiments can be designed. Scientists competing to prepare R & D proposals in response to Government contracts – experimenting with actual situations. Scientists may be competing to prepare R & D proposals in response to Govt contracts, experimenting with actual situations.

Psychometric Method

Psychometric tests are a standard and scientific method used to measure individual's mental capabilities and behavioral style. They are designed to measure candidate's suitability for a role based on the required personality characteristics and aptitude (or cognitive abilities). They deal with individual development potential, like attitude and skills tests, teambuilding potential – personality and attitude tests, leadership development potential – skills, personality and attitude tests, advancement and succession planning- aptitude, attitude and personality tests. There are a number of studies dealing with this subject in full like the one by L.R. Price (2016) In the context of the psychometric methodology application in Library and Information Science two important topics in scientific information use are studied: (1)Motivation, and (2) Cognitive Organization.

Motivation is the force that initiates, guides and maintains any goal- oriented behavior. In the context of Information Use studies, Motivation deals with why information is sought? (Farhadpoor. M R. 2017). There can be different motives for information use. They are:

- Achievement motive;
- Curiosity motive;
- Self evaluative motive;
- Affiliation motive;
- Utility motive (cash/reward);
- Ego motive.

Own statement of motives is difficult to validate.

Cognitive Organization

German Psychologist, Ulric Neisser is considered the father of cognitive psychology. With the publication of his book *Cognitive Psychology* (1967) Neisser brought together research concerning perception, pattern recognition, attention, problem solving, and remembering. Researchers working on problems throughout the field saw a unified theory that connected their research to this approach. Cognitive psychology is the scientific study of mental processes such as "attention, language use, memory, perception, problem solving, creativity and thinking"(American Psychological Association (2013). German Psychologist Wolfgang Kohler (1947) expanded the Gestalt principle of perceptual and cognitive organization to the province of memory and learning by assuming that recognition and recall are functionally another case of grouping and when a form or pattern is perceived it tends to be subsequently recognized and recalled in a well-structured, organized way; memory traces in the brain are conceived of as neuro-physiological correlates of recognition and racall. Recently, cognitive psychology has been influenced by approaches to information processing and information theory developed in computer science and artificial intelligence.

In the context of Library and Information Science research in User Studies the problems studied are various, like:

- How do scientists approach to locate the desired information?
- The pattern of approach in information search by individual user would match with one's habit of cognitive organization.
- Using of many headings to locate the desired information rather than the few presented by classification scheme/ thesaurus, etc.
- The pattern will lead to re-designing of the systems.

- Pattern of verbal association through computerized content analysis.

Computer-based Research

Computer is an essential tool for research, whether for academic purpose or for commercial purpose. Computers play a major role today in every field of scientific research from genetic engineering to astrophysics research. It led the way to a globalized information portal that is the World Wide Web. There is hardly anything that is not available on the Internet.

According to J. C. Modh (2014) research process consists of series of actions or steps necessary to effectively carry out research and the desired sequence of these steps. The following order concerning various steps provides a useful procedural guideline regarding the research process: (1) formulating the research problem, (2) Extensive literature survey, (3)developing the hypotheses, (4) preparing the research design, (5) determining sample design, (6) collecting the data, (7) execution of the project, (8) analysis of data, (9) hypotheses testing, (10) generalization and interpretation, and (11) preparation of the report or presentation of the results, i.e. formal write-up of conclusions (Kothari, C.R.2004). There are five major phases of research process. They are: Conceptual phase, Design and Planning Phase, Data Collection phase, Data Analysis phase, and Research Publication phase. In all these phases, computer has a definite role to play. Perhaps the most important role of computers is in data analysis wherein Software like SPSS and spreadsheets are widely used. It provides analysis facilities like the following and many more: statistical inferences, correlation & regression analysis, analysis of variance, multivariate data analysis, frequency distribution, data exposition by using various graphs like line, scatter, bar, ogive, histogram, pie chart, etc.

Online systems can give opportunities to observe information seeking behaviour of scientists more accurately, unobtrusively, measurably, tabulated data, and undefiably. Further, it can provide immediate feedback. Computer assisted research provides exciting potential for psychometric researches.

IMPACT OF USER STUDIES

User Studies have been Influencing directly or indirectly modern library operations and services. They have particular impact on the following:

1. Collection development in maintaining a balanced and appropriate collection, in always satisfying users' interests;
2. Weeding out of books – unused books/dead stock;
3. Resource Allocation – resources of materials, finance, manpower, physical facilities, etc;
4. Improvement of library techniques, on the basis of proper catalogue use studies, classification and its effectiveness, etc.
5. Development of user-based information services;
6. Developing appropriate and innovative user education programmes.

PATTERNS OF USER BEHAVIOUR

Some important Findings from User Studies relating to the patterns of user behaviour as are listed by P.S. Kawatra (1992) are worth stating:

1. Users of information belong to identifiable groups with characteristic patterns of information requirements.
2. The role of the user is an important determinant of information need.
3. Accessibility is a key factor determining the use of an information source.

4. The user's awareness of and ability to use, information sources is often imperfect.
5. Interpersonal communication is one of the most important means of transmitting information.
6. The amount of information required varies considerably between persons.
7. Users often require information to be supplied at short notice.

REFERENCES

ALLEN, Thomas John (1965), "Sources of ideas and their effectiveness in parallel R & D projects", *Paper presented at the Second ONR Conference on Research Program Effectiveness, Washington D. C. July 28, 1965*; Cambridge , Mass, MIT

AMERICAN PSYCHOLOGICAL ASSOCIATION (2013), *Glossary of Psychological Terms...*

BERNAL, J.D. (1948), "Preliminary Analysis of Pilot Questionnaire on the Use of Scientific Literatures", Paper submitted to the Royal Society Scientific Information Conference, 1948.

CHAMBANLAL, Modh Jatinkumar (2014) "Role of Computer Applications and Tools in the Scientific Research Process" *International Journal of Research in Science and Technology* Vol. 3 (V), October-December, 2014.

COMTE, Auguste (1853), The Positive Philosophy of Auguste Comte, 2 volumes, tr. by H. Martineau; Chapman (re-issued by Cambridge University Press, 2009).

CRUZ (The Centre for Research on User Studies), British Library Research and Development Division, Sheffield (1975)

CUSHING, Frank Hamilton, etc, (1990), *Cushing at Zuni; the Correspondence and Journals of Frank Hamilton Cushing, 1879-1884,* University of New Mexico Press, 1990.

CUSHING, Frank Hamilton (1990) *My Adventures in Zuni*, Pamphlet, ISBN 1-121-39551-1.

DEVARAJAN, G. (1995), *Library Information User and Use Studies,* New Delhi, Beacon Books

FARHADPOOR, Mohammad Reza, (2017) *A study of Users' Motivation in using Information Services of Regional Information Center for Science and Technology,* Business.

GARFIELD, Eugene (1955). "Citation Indexes for Science: A New

Dimension in Documentation through Association of ideas" *Science* 122 (3159), July 15,1955 Pp.108-111.

JENNINGS, H.H.(1987) *Sociometry in Group Relations,* 2nd ed, Westport, Greenwood.

KAWATRA, P. S. (1992), "Methods and Techniques of User Studies *in, Library user studies,* Bombay, Jaico Publ House,1992, Chapter 7, Pp.122-182.

KINCH, John W. *Ed.* (1971) *Sociology in the world of taday,* Massachusetts, Addison-Wesley Publishing Co.

KOHLER, Wolfgang (1947) , *Gestalt Psychology: An Introduction to New Concepts in Modern Psychology,* New york, Liveright.

KOTHARI, C.R. (2004) *Research Methodology, Methods and Techniques,* New Age International Publishers, Pp,10-19, 2004.

MALINOWSKI, Bronislaw (1929) The Sexual Life of Savages in North Western Menalesia, New York, Halcyon House.

MENZEL, Herbert (1966). "Information Needs and Uses in Science and Technology" in the *ARIST 1966*

MORENO, Jacob L. (1934) *Who shall survive? A New approach to the Problem of Human Interrelations, Washington D.C., Nervous and Mental Disease Publishing Co.*

MORENO, Jacob L.(1943) "Sociometry and the Cultural Order", *Sociometry* 6:299-344.

NEISSER, Ulric (1967) *Cognitive Psychology,* Appleton- Century Crofts, 1967.

PRICE, Derek J. de Solla, (1965), "Networks of Scientific Papers, the pattern of bibliographic references indicates the nature of the scientific research front", *Science;* 149 (3683), July 30, 1965 :510-515.

PRICE, Larry R. (2016), *Psychometric Methods: theory into Practice,* New York, Guilford Publications, 2016.

SHAW, Ralph R. (1956), *Pilot Study on the Use of Scientific Literature by Scientists,* Rutgers University, Dept of Library Science, 1956.

SMITH, William and Vickers, I. (1973) "Sociometric Choice in Small Group Communication", *Journal of Applied Communication Research,* 1(2):97-103, Summer 1973.

TREADWELL, T. et. al. (1998) *Computerised Sociometry,* 2nd ed, Western Chlester University, PA.

YANCEY, Rodney (2005): *Fifty Years of citation indexing and analysis,* Thompson scientific, 2005.

11
Economics of Information

According to Lionel Robbins (1935) *"Economics is a science which studies human behaviour as a relationship between ends and scarce means which have alternative uses"*. The basic problem is of economizing on the scarce resources; in other words, husbanding of resources. Information is recognized as a resource of the society and is therefore to be efficiently managed for the welfare of the society. The *Dictionary of Economics* by Graham Bannock, etc, (1997) defines economics as "*the study of the production distribution and consumption of wealth in human society*"

Economics of information (EoI) as a new phrase appeared only in the 1960s. The subject is dealt with in two different fronts:

1. Information and knowledge as a necessary input or influencing factor in different economic activities;
2. Information as a commodity which is amenable to the usual economic activities of production, distribution, consumption and various postulates,

theories and laws inherent therein.

Economics of Information and Knowledge is an emerging topic of interest for both economists and management scientists. The term began to appear in the terminology of economists only in the 1960s although the importance of information was recognized in market operations and competition, right from the time of Adam Smith (1776), the Father of Economics. Some of the others who wrote on Economics of Information from the side of economists are: G.J. Stigler (1961), Kenneth J. Arrow (1962), Fritz MachLup (1966), K.E. Boulding (1966), and J, Marshak (1968).

THREE AREAS OF ECONOMICS OF INFORMATION

E o I is presented in three separate but related contexts:

1. A definitional context in which information will be defined and its economic roles and economic properties are identified.
2. A macro-economic context in which the role of information in the structure of national economics will be described, and, to the extent possible, measured.
3. A micro-economic context in which the economic costs and values associated with information in specific forms will be identified and, to the extent possible, measured based on available data.

(*International Encyclopedia of Information Science*, 1997).

INFORMATION / KNOWLEDGE INDUSTRY

EoI is an established subdivision of economics that is concerned with the information industry. The founder of this specialism was Fritz MachLup (1902-1983). He devoted his life to the goal of assessing the growth of information industries. His pioneering book was *The*

Production and Distribution of Knowledge in the United States (1962). This has been a seminal contribution in establishing measures of the information society. He distinguished 5 broad industry groups which were broken into 50 sub-brands. These groups were: (a) Education (e.g. schools, libraries and colleges, (b) Media of Communication (e.g. Radio and television, advertising), (c) Information Machines (e.g. Computer equipment, musical instruments), (d) Information Services (e.g. law, insurance, medicines), (e) Other important activities (e.g. research and development, non-profit activities. He ascribed an economic value to each and found out its contribution to the Gross National Produce (GNP), He found that 29 per cent of US GNP in 1958 came from the knowledge industries. This was at that time a remarkable rate.

In 1960 Peter Drucker, the management guru, alerted that "Knowledge has become the foundation of the modern economy as we have shifted from an economy of goods to a knowledge economy"

In 1977 Marc Uri Porat brought out *The Information Economy: [.* Porat's study was more detailed and objective than that of MachLup. He therefore found out that 46 per cent of US GNP is accounted for by the information sector. So it was a rising trend of the information economy, from 29% in 1958 to 46% in 1977. Porat suggested that here are two information sectors: the Primary and the Secondary. In the primary sector knowledge industries manipulated knowledge and information to produce new knowledge products and services. In the secondary sector, knowledge and information manipulation was one part of material production processes information being utilized in the production and sale of material outputs and the provision of services. The Report claimed that when taken together these sectors accounted for over half of all economic activity in America. This was showing an increase in MachLup's figure, leading Porat to conclude that US was first becoming an information society. Around the same time as of Porat's Report, Daniel Bell (1974) came out with his work, *The Coming of Post-indiustrial Society* Bell suggested three more dynamics: (a) theoretical knowledge would become increasingly important (a change in the axial principle of society), (b) expectations about the future would foreground issues of technology, its control and potential for transforming existence, new decision making processes would appear. He argued that methods of organizing social activities (the manner in which decisions are reached) could be regarded as intellectual technologies which spread by example, successful techniques are copied by other actors and groups. Furthermore, the major source of structural change in society is the change in the character of knowledge, a change which substitutes "a technical order for the natural order".

KNOWLEDGE INDUSTRY PRODUCTS

"Information industry" and "Knowledge Industry" are almost synonymous terms. To be exact, "knowledge industry" can be used as a broader term as knowledge products and information products can be differentiated.

Knowledge industry can be defined as the whole range of commercial and industrial activities which underlie and facilitate the compilation, distribution, and sale of such products as books, databases and broadcasts. All organizations, media and formats which are capable of performing all or part of these functions are covered by the definition.

The primary producers of knowledge are individuals who generate it through intellectual creativity based on experimentation, empirical research, observation, experience, reading or imagination. The communication of this knowledge, except in the case of interpersonal communication, depends upon the infrastructural facilities provided by the knowledge industry from the creator to the consumer.

1. The knowledge industries are therefore the secondary producers of information. Among them the longest established are the Publishers. The role of the publisher is that of a capitalist and organizer of information. Practice of book publishing is more than 500 years old now. The work of the primary producer (author) is followed up by a process of editing, production, marketing, sales and distribution, A vast international industry has grown up around these processes.
2. Then there is the media organizers who are involved in the production of radio and television. They are larger than publishing houses because of the very high capital costs of production. There is more state involvement in this area, especially in broadcasting.
3. The final producer group of more amorphous, and increasing importance. They are the so called hosts who provide access to databases. They are not normally primary producers of these databases but their function is similar to that of the publishers of books, who provide the essential channel of communication connecting producers and end-users.
4. The cable-television operators provide access through wireless systems.

Typical products of knowledge industries include, various products and formats:

Products	**Formats**
Books	Print – Most common
Magazines	Mass media
Newspapers, Television &	Televisions –Terrestrial
Radio Programmes	Broadcasts
	Cable Television

Databases	Satellite Broadcasts, T.V., Teletext & Independent Systems TV Gateway to information services, websites and databases.

INFORMATION AS A RESOURCE

The emergence of Economics of Information (EoI) is consequent to the recognition (1) that Information is a Resource, and (2) that Information is a commodity. The first emerges from the importance of information in every human activity and in the sustenance and development of the society. Information is an universal all-pervasive phenomenon.

Information input is necessary in every individual or social activity, like;

Information in decision making,

Information in education,

Information in research and development,

Information in business and industry,

Information in the development of culture,

Information in international understanding,

Information in defense, war, diplomacy and peace,

Information in government and administration, and

Information in economic, political and social life of the individual.

There is this generalization then: "*Information is, therefore, an indispensable resource to the individual and to the society or nation*". Arising out of the above generalization is the axiom that "*whoever has the right information is the better off*". This we can call the Information Advantage.

Information supplements our skills, abilities, our income and savings, our welfare, etc. It is a natural complement to all individual resources. Hence it is wealth, or power, or property – something by the nature of its uses deserving to be acquired and possessed,

The state of being informed involves three pre-requisites:

1. The relevant information must exist in a suitable form,
2. He must know that it exists, and
3. He must know how to find and use It wisely and well.

We are not very often conscious of these conditions and, therefore, we do not develop a helpful attitude towards realization of the problems involved in being well informed.

If the first condition is to be fulfilled someone must collect and organize the relevant information, In the absence of that we, users, always try to put up with inadequate arrangements for information, say, we travel without maps, we invest without proper information, we do many things without information.

With regard to the second condition, until we know that information exists we tend to assume that information does not exist.

In the case of the third condition, we do not need the information badly enough to look for it, Indeed we may even use the outdated information or wrong information we have. We may also misuse the information we have, or we may ignore vital information. The result is that our decisions go wrong, because they are based on wrong, inadequate information.

SPECIAL IMPORTANCE OF SCIENTIFIC INFORMATION

Information is an essential resource for the individual and society, comparable to other resources like resources of nature – land, minerals and water, resources of capital, labour and intellectual manpower and human skills. This crucial importance of information or its indispensability demands that information has to be adequately produced, distributed and consumed, like any other essential commodity. If information is an indispensable resource for the society scientific information is a more vital resource, because today, science and society are so intertwined. The present society of ours is a scientific and technological society (Gray & Perry, 1975).

CONSEQUENCES OF THE IMPORTANCE OF INFORMATION

1. Information Industry : The vital realization of the importance of information led to the mergence of what is called the information industry. In the beginning it was only an area under occupation of scientific societies and organizations. Later, governments entered the field in a large scale. Still later, commercial agencies have entered the field. Corresponding to development of this information industry there has been increasing realization of the importance of information and its better use.

2. Information as a Factor of Production : Proper addition to information input will lead to increased productivity. It will increase the productive efficiency of labour and management through increased knowledge and skill. Finally, information can be used as a factor of production; and productivity measures can be worked out as in the case with the triad of production factors - land, labour and capital.

3. Economics of Information Provision : Resource allocation is a process and strategy involving a company or a government deciding where scarce resources should be used in the production of goods or services. Allocation refers to the relative division of the resource flow among alternative product uses. A good allocation is one that is efficient, i.e. that allocates resources among product and end-uses in conformity with individual preferences as weighted by the ability of the individual to pay. The policy instrument that brings about an efficient allocation is relative prices determined by supply and demand in competitive markets Daly H.E. (1'993). Resource allocation for information provision was a subject which won recognition for Nobel Prize award to Kenneth Arrow in 1972 for his contributions to general equilibrium analysis and welfare economics. What should be the optimal share of the resources of the society to be set apart for the information sector is the subject of enquiry.

4. Information Industry Share : Information industry's share in nation's economy has been an exercise of modern economists. For example was Fritz MachLup's study. MachLup (1962) studied the US economy in1958 and found that about 29 per cent of the GNP came from the knowledge industries. Similarly Marc Uri Porat (1977) after examining the U.S. economy found out that 46 per cent of US GNP was accounted for by the information sector.

5. Cost Analysis of Information Systems : The realization of the importance of information made it necessary to have some deliberate arrangements made for the storage and retrieval of information, by collecting, organizing, and making accessible the records of all relevant information. They are called Information Systems – libraries, documentation centres, information centres, information analysis centres, referral centres, information storage and retrieval systems, data bases and data banks, online library networks, etc, etc. are the various Information Systems (Gray & Perry, 1975).

In all kinds of organizations, may be industrial companies, government establishments, business firms, or research and development institutions increasing attention is being paid to the design and development of information systems to meet their complex information needs. The cost analysis of these information systems attracted the attention of information specialists and economists

COST ANALYSIS

Costing: Importance and Relevance

"*Costing is the classifying, recording and appropriate allocation of expenditure for the determination of the costs of products or services, and for presentation of suitably arranged data for the purposes of control, and guidance of management*" Wheldon (1975). The main aims of costing are cost control and improvement in efficiency. Cost accounting is a specialized branch of accounting that deals with the classification, recording, and allocation of current costs and prospective costs. In the modern commercial world, it is one of the most important techniques or process for a business.

The ability to cost activities has become more important today, because of

(a) the diminishing resources,

(b) the increased accountability,

(c) the more choices in methods of delivery, and

(d) continuing interest in charging and outsourcing.

An inherent problem for information managers is that information work is labour intensive with staff costs typically accounting for 35% -55% of the department costs. Short term budget adjustments are not possible because staff members are appointed on fixed time basis.

Methods of data collection

The possible data collection methods are:

- observation/scrutiny of records,
- work sampling,
- selective/continuos time logging,
- diary keeping/benchmarking

But these methods themselves are labour intensive. They may be de-motivating and ultimately counter productive.

- Attempts to control staff time too rigidly may inhibit initiative, reduce responsiveness, damage customer quality and customer relations.
- Amount of time likely to be required for professional updating and skills refreshment cannot be attributed to specific service costs.
- Costing is also complicated by the range of different elements that must be included to arrive at the total cost of a product or services especially when I T is involved where capital a and recurring costs of I T have to be apportioned (e.g. hardware, software, technical support, user documentation, etc.)
- Confusion arises often over the identification of fixed and variable costs, average and marginal costs, direct and indirect costs, treatment of organization overheads (cost of accommodation and utilities).
- Policy for depreciation of capital purchases such as work station and furniture.

ADVANTAGES/USES OF COSTING

- To decide between alternative methods of service delivery;
- To investigate the costs of new or improved service provision;
- To explore the scope for cost recovery and informed pricing decisions;
- To isolate costs of providing specific services and/ or serving particular customers;
- To prepare more accurate budget estimates and support funding bids;
- To demonstrate financial competence and improve credibility;

- To compare performance with peers or competitors;
- To measure efficiency and effectiveness;
- To satisfy internal and external audit; and
- To prove value for money.

CONCEPTS/ TERMS

Generally, costs can be considered in two main heads: direct costs and indirect costs.

Direct Costs : Those that are directly identified with a particular job, product, or process, for e.g. productive labour or materials which forms part of a product, such as binding a publication. Direct costs are known as *Prime Costs.*

Indirect Costs : Those costs of the business that cannot be identified with specific outputs, e. g, executive staff, or service /utilities which support production such as heating and lighting. indirect costs are also known as *Overhead Costs.*

There is another fundamental categorization of costs:

Variable Costs : Those which vary directly with changes in the level of an activity, e. g. materials consumed in delivering a service, such as paper in photo copying, but not necessarily the associated labour costs.

Fixed Costs : are costs that are not directly affected by changes in volume, but are incurred irrespective of activity level – at least in the short term (e.g. salaried operators, rent and rates). Fixed costs all become variable costs in the long term.

There are costs which do not conform neatly to this pattern:

Mixed /Costs : Costs that are those where there is a fixed amount of cost and also an element which varies with output e.g. for a telephone, the line rental is a fixed cost, but the call charges are variable. Mixed costs are also known as *Simi-Variable Costs.*

Stepped Costs : They are a category of fixed costs which vary with the level of output in large steps or jumps rather than proportionately to output, e.g. when demand for photocopying increases an additional machine is purchased, and the machine cost stay increased.

Full Costs : are figures representing a combination of the allocated direct costs and apportioned indirect costs of a product/service/take/unit (i.e. a combination of all the variable costs and an appropriate share of fixed costs. Full Costs are also known as *Total Costs.*

Marginal Costs : are increases or decreases in total costs that result when output is varied by one unit – i.e. the additional cost of the next unit of output. Marginal Costs are also known as *Incremental Costs.*

Unit Costs : represent the amount of resources used to produce one unit of a specified product or service based on the total cost divided by the total output over a period of time. These are also called *Average Costs.*

Cost drivers : are the factors that drive or cause consumption of particular costs.

Marginal Costing and Break Even Analysis : are used to analyze relationships between cost and volume and to determine the point at which a priced product or service covers its costs. Such techniques are often used for setting prices/charges, especially in a non-profit organization.

MAIN STEPS INVOLVED IN COSTING

1. Decide as to what should be studied; the focus and level of the costing exercise – the product, service, process or system which will be the subject of study or cost objective.
2. Determine a sensible activity or period base – unit measures of output, or time units (such as an hour, day, week, month, or year);

3. Identify all the relevant cost components; gather available data and plan how to collect data not readily available (such as staff time spent on various tasks);
4. Classify that cost according to their type – direct/indirect, fixed/variable – and establish behaviour pattern of variable and any stepped cost;
5. Calculate (via measurement or estimation) and allocate the direct costs;
6. Group or aggregate the indirect costs, on the basis of their homogeneity or similar casual relationships with the cost objective, to form *cost pools*;
7. Identify *cost drivers* as basis for relating costs to objectives, select method for (re)distributing overheads and apportion the indirect costs; and
8. Consolidate the data and choose a suitable form of presentation.

COSTING METHODS AND TECHNIQUES

There are various approaches to costing related to the above concepts which can be used to establish the costs of products and services. Your choice of method will depend on your purpose such as budget preparation, internal/external comparisons, or pricing decision.

COST - BASED BUDGETTING

The budgetary/financial requirements of an information product /service are to be identified under:

(a) Initial costs/for start up,

(b) Annual operating costs (Recurring Expenditure), and

(c) Future needs.

The following items have to be covered under the above three levels of expenses proposed/anticipated:

1. Facilities

(a) Initial costs: Preparation of space/building, reconstruction, renovation, new partitions, lighting, interior decoration, etc.

(b) Annual renovation needed,

(c) Future extension/new facilities.

2. Equipments and Furniture

(a) Initial costs – For purchase of new items.

(b) Annual costs – Repairs, renewals, replacements, additions, AMC, etc.

(c) Future costs – new equipments and new furniture.

3. Salaries and Wages

(a) Initial : Consultancy costs, etc,

(b) Annual: Salaries of professional, non-professional, clerical and manual staff.

(c) Future needs: Periodical rises, expansion of staff, salary revisions, etc.

4. Documents: (Books and Periodicals and Others)

(a) Initial costs: Purchase of a basic collection of books, journals, and secondary publications.

(b) Annual costs: Additions, Subscription for journals, networks, database access, etc,

(c) Future needs: Extension of the collection to new subject areas.

5. Materials, Supplies and Consumables

(a) Initial supplies.

(b) Annual expendables.

(c) Future: contingencies.

6. Miscellaneous

(a) Initial: Expenses of planning and setting up.

(b) Annual: Costs of travelling and conveyance, staff training, etc,

(c) Future: Evaluation costs at the close of a period.

The above items can be divided /consolidated under the following heads also:

A. Capital Costs,

B. Non-Recurring costs, and

C. Recurring costs.

COST-BENEFIT ANALYSIS

Cost-Benefit Analysis is used to determine the economic feasibility of a proposal by identifying both the monetary/financial, and opportunity/ social costs and benefits – to decide whether an activity/products/service is worth the "price", This type of analysis aims to evaluate both monetary and non-monetary/intangible costs and benefits, and can thus be distinguished from *Cost-effective studies*.

Cost-effective studies aim to maximize performance output in relation to input costs;

Cost-efficiency studies aims to minimize input costs.

THREE SECTIONS OF COST-BENEFIT ANALYSIS:

There should be three sections in cost-benefit analysis:

1. Costs,
2. Benefits, and
3. Return on Investment.

1. Costs

Costs occur in different areas mentioned earlier. They are:

(a) Facilities;

(b) Equipment & Furniture;

(c) Salaries & Wages,

(d) Documents;

(e) Materials & Consumables,

(f) Miscellaneous.

They can be grouped under:

(i) Capital Costs,

(ii) Other Non-Recurring Costs;

(iii) Recurring Costs.

(iv) Social Costs/ Opportunity Costs.

One more item needs to be reckoned with the Recurring Costs, i.e. the cost on the side of the users, for example, the time taken by users in obtaining a service or the *Opportunity/ Social Costs.*

2. Benefits

(a) Direct benefits or Savings : These are costs that are reduced or eliminated by the service/system, like:

- reduction in clerical/personal;
- elimination of some specific costs, like postage/ stationery; and
- reduction in cost due to improved procedures.

(b) Measurable benefits : These are money accruing to the institution through some features of the system/ product/service

= Cost gains through speed and accuracy.

(c) Intangible benefits : Certain advantages are difficult to evaluate in term of money

= Better information leading to better decisions which in turn leading to greater efficiency.

(d) Benefits to the Users and the Society :

= Elimination of time delay/cumbersome procedures;

= Savings in money/fees/expenses;

= Social /individual opportunities for information advantage.

3. Return on Investments

Once costs and benefits are studied the crucial part of the analysis is to know whether the system/product/ service is worthwhile. The *Pay-back Time* when the product brings back the money invested, and the *Break–even analysis* to determine the point at which a priced product/ service covers its costs are used here to evaluate the economies of the product/service.

REFERENCES

ARROW, Kenneth J.(1962),"Economic Welfare and the Allocation of Resources for Invention" *in The Rate and Direction of Inventive Activity; Economic and Social Factors,* ed by N.R. Nelson, National Bureau of Economic Research, Princeton University Press, Pp.609-26, 1962.

BELL, Daniel (1974) *The Coming of Post-Industrial Society,* New York, Harper Colophon Books

BOULDING, K.E. (1966) "The Economics of Knowledge and the Knowledge of Economics", *American Economic Review,* Vol. 56 no.2, 1966 Pp.1-13.

DALY, Herman E. (1993) "Allocation, Distribution, and Scale towards an economics that is efficient, just, and sustainable" *Ecological Economics* 6:185-193.

DE RUS, Gines (2010), *Introduction to Cost-Benefit Analysis for Reasonable Shortcuts,* 5th edn, U.C. Berkeley, Worth Publishers.

DICTIONARY OF ECONOMICS, by Graham Bannock, etc, (1997)

DRUCKER, Peter, (1969) *The Age of Discontinuity....*

GRAY, John and PERRY, Brian, (1975), *Scientific Information* AGRIS, Information Systems Division, National Agricultural Library, Washington D.C.

INTERNATIONAL ENCYCLOPEDIA of Information Science (1997) ed. By John Feather and Paul Sturges.

MACHLUP, Fritz (1962) *Production and Distribution of Knowledge in the United States,* Princeton University Press.

MARSHAK, Jacob (1968) "Economics of Inquiring, Communicating, Deciding", American Economic Review, Vol 58 no.2, 1968 Pp.1-18.

MISHAN, E. J. (2007), *Cost-Benefit Analysis*, 5th edn, U.C. Berkley, Worth Publishers.

PORAT, Marc Uri (1977), *Information Economy; Sources and Methods for Measuring the Primary Information Sector (Detailed Industry* Reports), Washington D.C., U.S. Dept. of Commerce).

ROBBINS, Lionel (1935), *An Essay on the Nature and Significance of Economic Science*: London, Macmillan & Co.

SMITH, Adam (1776) *An Enquiry into the Nature and Causes of the Wealth of Nations,* 2 Vols, W. Strahan T. Cadell, London.

STIGLER, G. J. (1961), "The Economics of Information", *Journal of Political Economy,* Vol. 69 Pp.213-25, 1961.

WHELDON, Harold J., *Wheldon's Cost Accounting and Costing Methods,* 13th Edn, by L.W.J. Owler and J..L. Brown, London, Macdonald & Evans, 1975.

12
Information Marketing

Information marketing is a field of study concerned with the application of the modern marketing concepts, principles, techniques and strategies in the management of Libraries and Information Centres with special emphasis on the marketing of their products and services. The subject takes into account the unique nature, properties and characteristics of information as a commodity or a marketable product.

WHAT IS MARKETING?

Marketing is not just selling. It is much more than that. Sale is only one of the different activities coming under marketing. (Coote & Bachelor, 1997). The difference between 'marketing' and 'selling' can be simply put as "*you sell what you have and you market what the buyer needs*".

The two professional definitions of 'marketing' are given here (Rowley, 2001, P. 3):

"*Marketing is the management process which*

identifies, anticipates, and supplies customer requirements efficiently and profitably" (Chartered Institute of Marketing).

"Marketing is the process of planning and executing the conception, pricing, promotion and distribution of ideas, goods and services to create, exchange and satisfy individual and organizational objectives" (American Marketing Association).

This American definition, on a closer analysis is found to emerge the following two statements (Rowley, 2001, P..2).

"Marketing is concerned with encouraging people to buy things that they really need or want, and interfering with people's behaviours, attitudes and values".

"Marketing is designed to bring you the products you want, when you want them, where you want them, at prices you can afford, and with the information that is necessary to make informed and satisfying customer choices

Rowley (2001, P.2-4) has also brought out 5 key aspects of marketing as emanating from the two professional definitions. They are:

1. *'Marketing is a business process'.*
2. *'Marketing is about meeting customer requirements'.*
3. *'Marketing meets the organization's objectives by assisting the organization to fulfil customer requirements efficiently and profitably'.*
4. *'Marketing is an exchange process'...* where the organization offers a product or a service against a sum of money.
5. *'Marketing applies to ideas, goods and services, referred to by the generic term 'product''.*

All organizations committed to customer requirements have to shape their activities and strategies with a *marketing orientation.*

INFORMATION AS A PRODUCT

While we say 'information marketing' the basic assumption is that information is a product worthy of the techniques, strategies and operational processes of modern marketing. What then is a 'product'?. A product has been defined by Kotler (2000) as follows:

"A product is anything that can be offered to a market for attention, acquisition, use or consumption that might satisfy a want or need. It includes physical objects, services, persons, places, organizations, ideas, experiences, events, properties, and information". (Kotler, 2000, P.394).

Another definition of a product given by Brassington & Pettit (1997) is also worth quoting:

"A product is a physical good , service, idea, person or place that is capable of offering tangible and intangible attributes that individuals or organizations regard as so necessary, worthwhile or satisfying that they are prepared to exchange money, patronage or some other unit of value in order to acquire it".

Apparently, the distinctive attribute of a 'product' is that it involves exchange of some value or money while offering or acquiring it. Thus a product has always an economic property.

Information as a product has the basic economic property, and much more than that. As a product information displays some distinct nature and properties. This aspect was brought out by Jennifer Rowley (2001) with due reference to Eaton and Bowden (1991). These special characteristics of information are examined in Section 1.3 below.

UNIQUENESS OF INFORMATION PRODUCTS

Compared to other products, information products have some distinct features. Eaton & Bowden (1991) have summarized some of the special characteristics of information. Similarly, Freiden, et al (1998) argue that the unique nature of information as a product demands a new approach to marketing and that distinguishes information marketing. The following are the unique characteristics of information as a product:

1. The contextual value of information : The economic value of information is not that readily quantifiable as in other products. Information has no intrinsic value; its value depends upon context and user. The same information may have different values for different users.

2. Reproducibility and multiplicity of information: Information is never lost when it is given to others. It does not diminish when consumed. Modern information technology adds boundless dimensions to the reproducibility and multiplicity of information as a product.

3. Interactivity of information : Unlike other commodities information is not always acquired for using in its original form, but it may be integrated with information from other sources and used as an input for producing new information products or services.

4. Repackageability of information : One and the same information can be produced and distributed in variant formats to different target groups to meet different requirements. Thus several different products or services can be generated out of one and the same original information to the extent that it becomes difficult to distinguish the original from the duplicate. Also one and the same original information may become available in different sources, often as repackaged products.

5. Technology bound delivery of information : Information delivery is closely bound with technology, which facilitates as well as constrains information transfer. Advent of the new information technology with its unprecedented achievements in communication systems, computer technology and digital transmission has now provided boundless opportunities for information transfer to individuals, workplaces and organizations in myriad forms of information products and services.

6. Perishability of information : Not all the information has an equal life span. Some information may be short lived and even perishable. Speedy delivery and timely use are decisive in maintaining the economic value of information as a product. Otherwise such information will go obsolete. At the same time some information can have multiple life cycles as ideas come into, move out of, and finally come back into fashion (Rowley, 2001, P. 84; Cronin & Gudim,1986).

7. Homogeneity of information : Commodities in business do have a great degree of homogeneity because they are mostly produced in bulk, but information services have a personal element in its production and delivery in order to be effective. For example, copies of books, journals, and other published records are identical, whereas an archival record or a manuscript document is unique. Information marketing has to deal with information pertaining to both extremes in terms of homogeneity.

8. Inseparability and inappropriability of information : Normally, a commodity in business passes through several hands between its manufacture and sale. In such cases, the possession of the physical good involved in the business transfers hands from one to another until it is finally received by the consumer. When publications do conform to this trade practice, information services do not. In information marketing, when changing hands all the intermediaries may retain the information so transferred. This is the inseparability of information as a product. This is also the inappropriability of information. Information, other than in its recorded form like a book, journal, CD-ROM, etc., is not fully appropriable as it cannot be removed from the mind of the seller when it is sold to a buyer. Information is thus inseparable from its source. Information is not lost when it is given or sold to others. Also, information is not fully appropriable by the buyer as in the case with any other commodity.

9. Tangibility of information : Tangibility is the quality of a commodity which can be physically experienced by anyone, like being heard, seen, felt, tasted, smelt, etc. Such goods can be legally taken as tangible assets. Information in fact is mostly intangible. It cannot be physically experienced as described above. But there is a tangible element in information and that corresponds with the medium of transfer. For example, information products like books and periodicals are tangible although the information that they contain is not (Rowley, 2001, P. 84).

10. Information, especially electronic information, may be acquired either by purchase or lease, or accessed online. Also, one and the same information can have multiple buyers while each one is having a chosen mode of acquisition with its own terms and conditions of sale or use.

11. Marketing of information may involve revealing the information at the stage of demonstrating the product which means the virtual exchange of the product may be made even before the contract of sale is entered into.

MARKETABILITY OF INFORMATION

As already stated, the basic assumption in 'Information Marketing', is that 'Information' is a product worthy of marketing'. Any product or service can be marketed provided it has the economic property, i..e. a value in terms of money or money's worth. Libraries and information centres are mainly dealing in the recorded information and hence "information marketing" in their context should mean marketing of the various information products and services they generate, manage and distribute by using the recorded information.

Why Marketing of Information?

Libraries and information centres have been traditionally engaged in serving the society by providing documents and information that individuals and organizations need or want for various purposes. These services were mostly free and were generally passive, that is, only in response to expressed demand. But due to the rising professionalism in library management new and more aggressive services came to be offered, both in anticipation and on demand. Along with growing dimensions of information requirements of the society more specialized products and services began to be offered. In this context, marketing concepts and techniques also began to be introduced in libraries and information management.

Many reasons are there why information products and services should be deliberately marketed:

1. Libraries and Information Centres do have to spend considerable amount of their time, money and expertise in the design and production of various information products/ services. This they do in anticipation of use by their clientele. But, repeated use of the same product/service will depend upon the quality of the product/service and also on efficiency of its distribution.
2. Both production and distribution of information products/services incur considerable costs. Over and above the capital and recurring (operational) costs to the library, the social costs also have to be accounted in the cost-benefit analysis of any information product/service.
3. Information is an advantage for the user and it has real value for the user depending upon the use made of it. Users are, therefore, often willing to pay for information served to them, depending on its quality, content, timeliness and exactitude.

4. If information has to be sold out and cost realized by the library their products/services have to be more user-oriented or need-oriented. For this, they must be designed and produced with the proper involvement of users. Further, information has to be served adequately and appropriately. For this, appropriate marketing strategies have to be designed and developed.
5. Some users at least are earning money by selling the information they freely collect through library and information services. They are especially the information brokers, and consultancy services. Therefore, there is a good reason behind charging the users for information so served to them, as realizing the cost from these users will go to make the product/service self-sustaining.
6. Fee-based services will be an additional revenue for the library for its further development. Especially in the context of the present economic recession and consequent budget cuts the income generated from services will be a great relief.

The above described details must serve as the essential background in which information marketing is to be examined. This does not, and need not, have to interfere with the free services now being given out from libraries. On the other hand, information marketing is concerned with the various fee-based library services only. There is, of course, the need for discretion and prudence on the part of the library management to decide what all services should be paid for and what all should be free. The golden rule here is: "*Does the user make or save any money with the information*?". We may come back to this point later.

MARKETING CONCEPTS

Zachert & Williams (1992) has identified and listed the Key Marketing Concepts as follows:

Market Segmentation and Quantification;

Market positioning including prioritizing clients and policy making;

Consumer analysis involving the information offering and quantification;

Market programme including market mix, placing, quantification and co-ordination; and

Marketing audit including information gathering, quantification, making judgements, and reporting.

MARKETING STRATEGY

There need be a clear Marketing Strategy for information marketing. Marketing Strategy is nothing else than a systematic marketing approach to matters pertaining to planning, production and distribution of products/services. Such an approach would basically consist of the following actions:

1. Identification of the target customers or user groups;
2. Determination of their needs;
3. Designing of services/products appropriate to their needs and at a fair price;
4. Costing the product/service and planning the resources;
5. Choosing the right type of distribution channel;
6. Necessary promotional or advertising work; and
7. Feedback and evaluation of products and services.

MARKETING STAGES AND STEPS

Marketing involves three Stages of activities, viz. Planning, Implementation, and Evaluation, and each of these Stages has different steps, as listed below:

Stages	Steps
Planning	Market Segmentation
	Product Development
	Promotion
	Distribution
	Pricing
	Evaluation
Implementation	Review of Market Plan
	Schedule Specification
	Resource Mobilization
	Staff and User Education and Training
	Promotional Activities
	Monitoring
Evaluation	Objectives
	Products
	Performance
	Distribution Channels

SETTING THE MARKET OBJECTIVES

Normally, the objectives of marketing can be set as follows:

(a) Facilitating better information transfer;

(b) Enhancing the use of information products and services;

(c) Facilitating production of more user-oriented rather than producer– oriented products;

(d) Generating resources for running information services.

(e) Enhancing the market share of particular products or organizations;

(f) Increasing the profitability;

(g) Getting established in the market place; and

(h) Maximizing the revenue.

Marketing objectives of any library or information centre must first of all be closely linked with the corporate objectives, i.e. the objectives of its parent institution. They must relate to what are to be achieved through strategic marketing.

MARKET RESEARCH AND SEGMENTATION

This activity involves the identification of users and target groups. Both actual and potential users have to be identified and their needs have to be assessed. This would require collection of information on the institutional projects/programmes as well as the individual user's interests and needs. Knowledge of the actual and potential market share of one's own products/services as well as of the competitors in the market is very important. For this purpose, *User Studies* have to be systematically designed and meticulously conducted.

Every such user study should have clearly defined objectives, decisions regarding the variables to be studied, the model to be followed, the population sample to be covered, the data to be collected, the data collection methods to be employed, and the analytical methods to be adopted. The results of such user studies have to be suitably categorized for fixing the type of service /product required for meeting the various needs. *User needs* may have to be analysed and categorized according to their nature and purpose, for example, as

Functional Needs being task- related information;

Problematic Needs arising from problem situations, *Social Needs* due to social and/or organizational needs,

Emotional Needs arising from emotional attachment of individuals to particular disciplines, authors, institutions, etc, and

Epistemic Needs arising from curiosity or desire of the individual for knowledge outside their own job areas.

Similarly *User Categories* also have to be identified

and their needs separately assessed. For example, in universities Students, Teachers, Researchers, and General academicians will be there, whereas in industrial or scientific organizations there are the Top Management, the R & D Staff, the Middle Managers, and the Technicians as the evident user categories. Finally, the specific services/products need be identified and listed as the choice/priority of each user group surveyed. Market research necessarily involves consumer analysis at depth so as to determine the needs and preferences of the present and potential clientele. This is known as *market positioning* wherein priority of clients, groups and information products/services are fixed through policy making.

PRODUCT DEVELOPMENT

This is the second Step in planning. Based on the information collected in market research, two decisions may have to be taken by library management:

(a) who should be the target group?; and

(b) what should be the product/service?.

Designing and developing of the product have to be in the light of many salient factors. The following is only a checklist of those parameters:

- type of library/information centre;
- user categories and their requirements (choices/priorities);
- use put to the information accessed by users;
- purpose for which the information is sought (like knowledge/education/current awareness/productivity/problem solving/ decision making/adaptation, etc.);
- sources of information;
- content aspects (like technical sophistication, currency, quality and accuracy, editorial qualities,

etc.);

- presentation of information (textual/non-textual);
- Format of Presentation;
- Coverage and scope (subject and period covered);
- periodicity;
- Distribution/audience targeted;
- Pricing and promotion;
- Manpower requirements (Knowledge and skill required, number of persons with specific knowledge or skill);
- Managerial considerations (feasibility, phases of development);
- Costs (start up costs, operational costs, reimbursable and non-reimbursable costs;
- Resources and facilities and ease of availability (like funds, manpower, information sources, materials, etc.);
- Length of start up time and gestation period (training required);
- Extent of disturbance causing to existing organizational structure including displacement of personnel, etc.);
- Finance (revenue and expenditure);
- Technology and its utilization (computer, communication and reprography equipments and facilities);
- Package media (print/audio-visual /demonstrations, interpersonal contacts, etc.).

TARGETING THE PRODUCTS

Targeting is adjusting the product to correspond well with customer needs in different stages of their diffusion process. The target user groups and the appropriate product mix to be developed should be decided. Planning should be done for every individual information service/ product separately, after taking into account all the parameters listed above including packaging/repackaging and even naming of that product. The product once designed and developed may have to be modified if the situation warrants.

PROMOTION

Promotion is the third Step in the Planning. Promotion involves mechanisms by which the target groups are duly informed about the products/services offered by the library/information centre. The threefold purpose of promotion are: *to communicate, to convince* and *to complete*. Decisions on the following have to be taken during the promotion Step:

The audience : to whom are we addressing the promotional materials?;

The message : what is the message sought to be communicated?

(to draw attention to?/

to provide information?/

to persuade?)

The channel : What are the promotional mechanisms available?

Which is the best? What are the alternatives?

The medium : What are the points to be considered in the design of promotional packages?

What alternatives are there?

What resources are necessary for each?

The personnel : What is the role of the library/ information centre staff in promotional activities?

PROMOTIONAL MECHANISM

Different mechanisms can be used for promoting information products and services. Besides oral campaigns and direct contacts with individuals there are several other direct and indirect methods for contacts with target groups. Indirect contacts are tried to be established through brochures, pamphlets, posters, guides, handbooks, newspaper releases, advertisements, tape-slide shows, video and radio transmission, newsletters, press releases, etc. Then, there are the exhibitions and demonstrations and various user education programmes specially organized for this purpose.

MARKETING IN THE DIGITAL AGE

Traditional marketing concepts and practices may not have full relevance in the modern digital age context. What is ideal is a practically good mix of the old and the new. While the concepts, principles and approaches may remain mainly the same certain strategic variations may have to be adopted in the light of the new possibilities advanced by modern digital environment. While traditional approaches were mostly intended for homogenous groups of customers the digital environment promises more individualistic, pin-pointed and expeditious services with immediate interaction, feedback and improvement possibilities. In other words, services of the library / information centre can be more user-centric than ever before. This rapid transition from a macro-environment to a micro-environment in marketing is the result of the digital revolution in communication. There are new ways of reaching potential buyers. Manesh Kumar & K. P. Singh (2015) writes: "*To accomplish the library mission and vision, social media is the soul of library marketing strategy and that it is how connecting the whole world in the web of information sharing*". Social Media possibilities are Face book, WhatsUp, Wilkis, Videos, PINTEREST, Google+, FOURSQUARE, Blogs, Twitter, library websites, LibGuides, GoodReads, Library Thing, and several others.

DISTRIBUTION

Distribution is the fourth Step in Planning. In this step the important decision to be taken is about the channels for distribution of information products and services. Since each channel has its own merits and demerits, as far as possible, a judicious mix of different channels should be used. The following are pointed out to be the options available for distribution:

- Interpersonal delivery;
- Group delivery (at meetings, conferences, seminars, user education programmes, demonstrations, etc,);
- Strategic placement of products at some noticeable locations;
- In-house dissemination (through reference or referral services);
- Local depositories (through co-operative arrangement with other libraries /information centres);
- Mass media (newspapers, journals, magazines, TV, radio, etc.);
- Postal delivery (mailing of products to individuals and institutions);
- Mobile phones and social media including all audio and video expositions listed earlier and many others like YouTube, WhatsAp, Instagram, LinkedIn, etc.
- and computer networks.

PRICING

Pricing is the final Step in Planning. Pricing of information products and services is now a very delicate issue as so long library services were free and common to all. Pricing has become necessary for the following reasons:

(a) There is now an increasing emphasis on accountability and self-sufficiency in relation to the resources utilized by libraries;

(b) The cost of information services/products is increasing steadily and there is the desirability of recovering costs as much as possible;

(c) There is also a special reason. The information brokers and consultants are usually charging high fees from their clients while they are often using the free services of the libraries and information centres.

(d) As a general rule, customers value what they pay for, and pay for what they value. They are willing to pay for the services they take from others. Therefore, every resistance against priced services will be soon disappearing if we are able to establish our product or service as having significant value to customers.

HOW ARE PRICES FIXED?

Pricing of products must be mainly based on costs incurred. Here, the following questions need be answered:

1. What are the costs involved in the generation of service/ product?
2. What factors /parameters need be considered in arriving costs?
3. What of these factors can be overlooked or ignored for costing and why?
4. Should the information service/product be given free of charge?
   — if so, to whom and why?
5. What should be the impact in relation to value of product, if given free?
6. If the services/products are to be charged for, what should be the criteria for pricing?
   — Full cost recovery?/Marginal or partial cost recovery?
7. Should variable prices be based on ability of the user to pay?
   — Should a profit percentage be added to cost in pricing?

8. Who all should be charged?
   — Internal clientele or external clientele, or both?
9. What should be the impact on users in relation to pricing of products?
   — Would they be willing to pay?
   — Would demand fall and in what extent, if product are priced?

MARKETING MIX

The success of any marketing strategy depends to a great extent upon the choice and application of a proper 'marketing mix'. To quote de Saez, (2003, P. 51) "*The marketing mix is the planned package of elements that makes up the product or service offered to the market. It is aimed at supporting the library and information service to reach target markets and specified objectives*". Marketing mix is an integral part of good marketing planning which in turn must depend on systematic environmental scanning, market research, understanding of users/ readers/ clients, and offering them quality products and services. Marketing mix, as a substantial part of any effective marketing strategy, is a combination of various elements that go to determine the product in relation to a chosen market place and target audience. It was Neil Borden (1965) who came forward with a model of Marketing Mix for use in market research, which had only three elements (3 P's), viz. *People, Physical evidence*, and *Process*. But the first classic model of the Marketing Mix was presented by McCarthy (1978) as the 4 P's, viz. *Product, Price, Place,* and *Promotion*. McCarthy had admitted that his classic model of the 4 P's was a development of a theory put forward by Neil Borden. Philip Kotler (1986) had earlier expanded the classic 4 P's (*product, price, place, promotion*) to include *power* and *public relations*. He introduced also '*mega marketing*' as a new term in marketing discipline. However, in the matter of the Marketing Mix, librarians and information professionals later found it necessary to expand the model with additional elements, viz. *People, Physical evidence,* and *Process.* Thus, the model of Marketing Mix has come to be known as the 7 P's in Information Marketing. The elements of the model are once again listed and explained below (Rowley,2001, P. 4-8).

Product as an element in the marketing mix deals with the creation, development and management of products. Product decisions are to be taken primarily with a view to meet customer needs and wants. New innovative products must be introduced as and when found strategically significant. Products must have proven competitive advantage based on customer's choices and may lead to establishment and maintenance of a brand name.

Price is an important element in the marketing mix. It is the value obtained in exchange of the product. There are many factors that influence fixing of the product price. Once fixed, it has both economic and psychological values. It is also a competitive tool. Price can both attract and distract customers. Therefore, price has to be fixed logistically.

Place as an element in the mix stands for the right time and the convenient location, when and where, the products must be available. It is concerned with the consumer service/delivery points such as retail outlets. In the present digital age, information marketing has many new options facilitating desktop or even cell phone delivery of products.

Promotion as an element in the mix relates to activities used to inform individuals and groups about an organization and its products, as well as to engage in customer education wherever necessary. Here again, the digital age opportunities are numerous and challenging. Websites, notifications, announcements, e-mails, SMS and all avenues of social media can be put to effective use in information marketing.

People *as an* element in the marketing mix stands for the persons engaged in creating and delivering the product to the customers, and interacting with them. The human factor is predominant in any marketing activity and it is more so in information marketing. The quality of interaction has a direct relation with customer satisfaction. In a library or information centre, the attitude and responsiveness of the staff goes a long way in the acceptability of the product or service. The personal involvement of the library staff in a service episode in the library and the interpersonal dialogue with the customer will lead to the exact enunciation of the information problem of the customer and its appropriate solution. Any number of electronic gadgets will not be able to handle such situations as a conscientious human agency does. Moreover, human beings generally prefer to be addressed and served individually and personally rather than generally and mechanically.

Process as an element in the marketing mix relates to the manner in which the service is rendered to the customer which may involve his participation and interaction in the service process. More often this involves customer education, at least in the first occasion of service process. There are more of self-service environments today than a few years ago with the increasing trend of digital transmission of information products/services.The process of information delivery has to be easy, expedient, personal and responsive in the better interests of information marketing.

Physical evidence is the final element in the marketing mix. This is concerned with the creation and maintenance of inviting surroundings in which a service is delivered to the customer like the atmosphere, ambience, image and the design of premises, as a tangible clue to quality of service/product. The library or information centre should necessarily have an attractive building, which is conveniently situated and comfortably maintained. A major part of information products and services are library/centre bound where the customer comes personally to procure the product. How far good the library/information centre is maintained is the clear and disputed physical evidence of the marketing strategy of the library or information centre.

EVALUATION

Evaluation is the final Stage in Marketing and this involves separate evaluation based on (a) objectives, (b) products, (c) performance, and (d) distribution channel.

Once the marketing programme has been in operation for some time an evaluation of the entire marketing programme becomes necessary. Answers to the following questions must be found:

Are the objectives achieved? If not, why?

How good are the products? Can they be made more effective?

Can productivity be maximized?

How good is the overall performance of the marketing programme? What is the impact on user population? Are they satisfied?

Are the channels used appropriate to the products?

Is the promotional material appropriate? Are the messages reaching the user segments? What is the impact on use? etc.

In the words of Palmer (2001), "*the essence of quality delivery in the marketing of services is now crystallized in SERVQUAL, a quantitative technique for measuring service quality*". SERVQUAL was derived directly from the researches of Parameswaran and others (1985) who had identified some ten factors as parameters of quality of service. These factors are: *Access, Reliability, Credibility, Security, Customer expectations, Responsiveness, Courtesy, Competence, Communication, and Tangible evidence.*

INFORMATION MARKETING IN INDIA

Marketing of information products and services is in its infancy in India. This is in spite of the fact that Dr. S.R. Ranganathan, the Father of Library Science in India, had through his *Five Laws of Library Science* advocated for an aggressive type of Reference Service to library users which he described as a "sublimated salesmanship". (*Infoscience*, 2017). Nevertheless, selling information as a commodity of value was a concept not conceived that early in librarianship.

As on today, an introspection can reveal that there can be reasons for the backwardness of information marketing. Some of them are listed here:

(a) Confusion confounds Indian librarians about marketing. By and large they have taken marketing in its restricted sense of library promotion and publicity only.

(b) There is sheer lack of a definite policy of information marketing in India, both at the national and the local levels, in respect of end users, distribution, tariff, service, etc.

(c) There are not sufficient user studies in India to prove the benefits of information marketing. The available user needs assessment studies are inadequate due to either methodological deficiencies, or due to the fact that they are not carried out on a continuing basis.

(d) Proper market research and segmentation studies are lacking in India. In that situation, proper product development and targeting are not possible.

(e) Users' reluctance to pay for information services often result in the generation of inferior quality products only due to economic reasons.

(f) Studies for evaluating particular information products and services are usually not generated in India.

(g) Until recently, Information Marketing was not a subject of study in Indian library school curricula and consequently library personnel do not have any exposure to the potential benefits of marketing. One *British Library Report and Survey* (1992) concluded that in libraries "*there was a lack of knowledge and skills in marketing and related disciplines, although there was a thirst for knowledge about them.*"

(h) There can be various value-added information products that are very useful to customers. But these are not adequately identified, generated and marketed by libraries in India.

(i) Finally, information as a commodity is not considered that valuable by the public at large, and hence it gets only a low priority in the Indian society.

CONCLUSION

The future of Indian libraries and information centres seems to depend very much on marketing of information products and services. The depleting resources of the nation as a whole, and of many institutions in particular, warrant that specialized and value-added information products and services have to be planned, developed and marketed not only as self-sustaining projects but also for generating additional revenue for supporting more development programmes. For this purpose, first of all, what is necessary now is to develop a marketing culture among the practitioners of the library and information profession. Appropriate manpower development must be a basic requirement. Library schools in India should incorporate information marketing into their syllabi and make use of qualified and competent marketing experts as their resource persons until a new generation of LIS teachers become knowledgeable and competent in the marketing area.

Latest technologies such as Web 2.0 and mobile services have opened up new avenues to do marketing in efficient and cost-effective ways. What is required is adequate fund support. Marketing of digital services, relationship marketing strategies, user centric approach, marketing via websites, mobile phones, video and YouTube, collaborative efforts, etc. are practised widely in libraries of today.

REFERENCES

BORDEN, N.H. ('1965). "The concept of marketing mix" *in* Schwartz, G. (Ed), *Science in marketing,* Wiley, P.386-97.

BRASSINGTON, F. and PETTIT, S. (1997), *Principles of marketing.* London, Pitman Publishing).

BRITISH LIBRARY RESEARCH AND DEVELOPMENT (1992). *Sponsorship in libraries; Vp;.1: Report and Survey.* Aslib.

COOTE & BACHELOR (1997), *How to Market Your Library Service Effectively,* London, ASLIB,

CRONIN, B. and GUDIN, M. (1986). "Information and productivity: a review of research" *International Journal of Information Management,* 6(2):85-101

De SAEZ, Eileen Elliot (2001). *Marketing concepts for libraries and information services,* Edn.2, London, Facet Publishing, (Edn. 1 came out in 1993, LA.).

EATON, J..J. and BAWDEN, D. (1991). "What kind of resource is information?". *International Journal of Information Management,* 11, P. 156-65

FREIDEN, et al (1998), "Information as a product, not goods, not services" *Marketing Intelligence & Planning* 3:1-13

INFOSCIENCE (2017). "Marketing information services; a conceptual framework", *Infoscience today,* November.*[http://www.infosciencetoday.org/type/articles/marketing-of-information-services-conceptual-_framework.html]*

KOTLER, Philip (1986). "Megamarketing". ", *Harvard Business Review,* March-April 1986, P.116-124

KOTLER, Philip (2000). *Marketing management: the millennium edition,* (Edn.10)

KUMAR, Manish and SINGH, Dr. K.P. (2015). "Marketing of library and information science products and services through social media – need of the hour", *Library Herald* , 53(4) December

McCARTHY, E. J. (1978). *Basic marketing ; a managerial approach* Edn. 6, Irwin Prentice-Hall

PALMER, A. (2001). *Principles of service marketing*, Edn. E3. McGraw-Hill.

PARAMESWARAN, A. et al (1985). "A conceptual model of service quality and its implications for future research", *Journal of marketing*, Fall Page 41-59.

RANGANATHAN, S. R. (1932), *Five Laws of Library Science,Madras Library Association.*

ROWLEY, J.A. (2001), *Information marketing*, Ashgate Publishing. ZACHERT & WILLIAMS (1992), Marketing Strategies for Information Services, Griffith

Bibliography

ALLEN, Agnes (1952), The Story of the Book, London, ...

ALLEN, Thomas John (1965), "Sources of ideas and their effectiveness in parallel R & D projects", *Paper presented at the Second ONR Conference on Research Program Effectiveness, Washington D. C. July 28, 1965*; Cambridge , Mass, MIT

ALLEN, T.J. (1968) *Aslib Proceedings* Nov.1968

AMERICAN PSYCHOLOGICAL ASSOCIATION (2013), *Glossary of Psychological Terms...*

AMERICAN SOCIETY FOR INFORMATION SCIENCE, ASIS-EIS Curriculum Committee (1974), *Continuing Library and Information Science Education: Final Report* by Elizabeth W. Stone, and Ruth J. Patrick (1974).

ARNOLD, S.E. (1990), "Marketing Electronic Information: theory, practice and challenges 1980-1990" *in ARIST Vol.25*, ASIS, Pp. 87-144.

RROW, Kenneth J.(1962),"Economic Welfare and the Allocation of Resources for Invention" *in The Rate and Direction of Inventive Activity; Economic and Social Factors*, ed by N.R. Nelson, National Bureau of Economic Research, Princeton University Press, Pp.609-26, 1962

AUGUSTINE, C.A. (2001), "Digital Revolution Syndrome and Libraries" *in* Devarajan, G. (ed). *New Challenges in Librarianship*, New Delhi, Ess Ess Publications, Pp. 12-28.

AUGUSTINE, C.A. (2005); "Economics of Information and Knowledge", *in* Devarajan, G. (Ed): *Library and Information Studies in the Digital Age (Professor K.A. Isaac Commemoration Volume)*, New Delhi, Ess Ess Publications,

2005, PP.1-30.

AUGUSTINE, C.A.(2015): "Social Informatics in LIS Research" *National Library Week 2015 KELPRO Souvenir* (Kerala Library Professionals' Organisation, Thiruvananthapuram,Pp.25-28

AUGUSTINE, C.A. (2018): "Information Economics: The New Name for an Old Subject.", *KELPRO Silver Jubilee Souvenir* (Kerala Library Professionals' Organisation (KELPRO), Thiruvananthappuram, Pp. 6-12.,

AUGUSTINE, C.A. (2019), "Information Economy" *in* Devarajan, G. (ed) : *Encyclopedia of Science of Information,* New Delhi, Ess Ess Publications, Pp.82-100.

AUGUSTINE, C.A. (2019), "Information Marketing". *In* Devarajan, G. (ed), *Encyclopedia of Science Information,* New Delhi, Ess Ess Publications,145-165.

BARKER, F. (1984) "Pricing Information Products" *Aslib Proeedings* 36(7/8), July-Aug P. 289-297.

BARNARD, C.C. (1938) "The selection of periodicals for medical and scientific libraries", *Library Association Record,* 40:549-57.

BELL, Daniel (1974) *The Coming of Post-Industrial Society,* New York, Harper Colophon Books

BERNAL, J.D. (1948), "Preliminary Analysis of Pilot Questionnaire on the Use of Scientific Literatures", Paper submitted to the Royal Society Scientific Information Conference, 1948.

BORDEN, N.H. ('1965). "The concept of marketing mix" *in* Schwartz, G. (Ed), *Science in marketing,* Wiley, P.386-97.

BORKO, H. "Information Science: What is it?", *American Documentation,* 1968 ,19(1):3-5.

BOULDING, K.E. (1966) "The Economics of Knowledge and the Knowledge of Economics", *American Economic Review,* Vol. 56 no.2, 1966 Pp.1-13.

BOULDING, K.E.(196). "Knowledge as A Commodity" *in Beyond Economics: Essays on Society, Religion and Ethics,* Michigan, University of Michigan, Press.

BRADFORD, S.C. (1934) "Sources of information on specific subjects", *Engineering* 137:85-86.

BRADFORD, S.C. (1948); *Documentation,* London, Crosby Lockwood & Sons, 1948

BRASSINGTON, F. and PETTIT, S. (1997), *Principles of marketing.* London, Pitman Publishing).

BRINDLEY, L.J. (1993), "Information Service And Information Product Pricing". *Aslib Proceedings* 45(11-12), Nov-Dec , Pp. 207-305.

BRITISH LIBRARY RESEARCH AND DEVELOPMENT (1992). *Sponsorship in libraries; Vp;.1: Report and Survey*. Aslib.

BROOKS, B.C. (1969) "Bradford's Law and the Bibliography of Science", *Nature* 224:953-956.

BROOKS, B.C. (1979) "The Bradford's Law: a new calculus for the social sciences?" *Journal of American Society for Information Science*, 30(4):233-54.

CASPER, Cheryl A. (1983), " Economics and Information Science" *In Information Science In Action: System Design*, ed. By Debons. London, Mauritius Nijhoiff Publishers, Pp.565-572.d by

CHAKRABORTY, A.R. , et. al. "Translations and Translation Services" *Annals of Library and Information Studies* Vol 22 (2) June 1975; P.60-72,

CHAMBANLAL, Modh Jatinkumar (2014) "Role of Computer Applications and Tools in the Scientific Research Process" *International Journal of Research in Science and Technology* Vol. 3 (V), October-December, 2014.

CHANDRATRE, Shripad, et. AL. (1998), *How To Market Your Library Service Effectively*, Edn. 2, London, Aslib Know How Series, ed by S.P. Welb.

CLODD, Edward (1938),*The Story of the Alphabet, New York...*

COLE, E.J. and EALE, N.B.J. (1917), *The history of comparative Anatomy, Part I : A statistical analysis of literature. Science Progress*11: April 1917.

COMTE, Auguste (1853), The Positive Philosophy of Auguste Comte, 2 volumes, tr. by H. Martineau; Chapman (re-issued by Cambridge University Press, 2009).

COMTE, Auguste, (1865), *A General View of Positvism (Discours sur l'ensemble du positivism, 1848*), tr. by J.H.Bridges, Trubner & co.

COOLEY, Charles Horton, Ed (1909). *Social Organisation; a study of the larger mind*, New York, Charles Scribners,The Mead Project.

COOPER, Michael D.(1973),"The Economics of Information" *in ARIST 1973 (Vol.8), American Society for Information Science, Pp.*

COOPER, Michael D. (1983), "The Structure and Future of the Information Economy" *Information Processing and Management,* 19(1):9-26.

COOTE, Helen (1997), *How to Market Your Library Service Effectively,* London, ASLIB Know How Guides,

CRONIN, B. (Ed) (1992), *The Marketing of Library and Information Services,* 2, Aslib Reader Series-4, (Edn. 1 1981), Associated Library.

CRONIN, B. and GUDIN, M. (1986). "Information and productivity: a review of research" *International Journal of Information Management,* 6(2):85-101

CRUZ (The Centre for Research on User Studies), British Library Research and Development Division, Sheffield (1975)

CUSHING, Frank Hamilton, etc, (1990), *Cushing at Zuni; the Correspondence and Journals of Frank Hamilton Cushing, 1879-1884,* University of New Mexico Press, 1990.

CUSHING, Frank Hamilton (1990) *My Adventures in Zuni,* Pamphlet, ISBN 1-121-39551-1.

DALY, Herman E. (1993) "Allocation, Distribution, and Scale towards an economics that is efficient, just, and sustainable" *Ecological Economics* 6:185-193.

DEBONS, Anthony (1988), *Information Science; an integrated view,* G.K. Hall & Co. Boston.

DEBONS, A and CAMERON, J, Eds. "Editorial Summary" *in* Perspectives of Information Science, the proceedings of the II NATO Advanced Study Institute, Wales, 1973.

DEBONS, A. and CAMERON, W.J.(1972), *Perspectives in Information Science; proceedings of the 1972 NATO Advanced Study Institute In Information Science,* University of Pittsburgh, USA.

DE FLEUR, M. L. (1966), De Fleur Model of Communication *jose.wordpress.com* by Dalu Jose 7 years ago.

DE FLEUR, Melvin Lawrence (1982), *Theories of Mass Communication,* Sandra Ball-Rokeach ,Longman,1982.

DENMAN, Frank, (1955), *The Shaping of the Alphabet, New York...*

DE RUS, Gines (2010), *Introduction to Cost-Benefit Analysis for Reasonable Shortcuts,* 5th edn, U.C. Berkeley, Worth Publishers.

DE SAEZ, Eileen Elliot (2001). *Marketing concepts for libraries and information services,* Edn.2, London, Facet Publishing, (Edn. 1 came out in 1993, LA.).

DEVARAJAN, G. (1995), *Library Information User and Use Studies,* New Delhi, Beacon Books

DEVARAJAN, G. (Ed.) (2001): *New Challenges in Librarianship,* New Delhi, Ess Ess Publications, 2001a.

DEVARAJAN, G. (Ed.) : (2005), *Library and Information Studies in the Digital Age (Professor K.A. Isaac Commemoration Volume),* New Delhi, Ess Ess Publications, 2005.

DEVARAJAN, G. Ed. (2019), *Encyclopedia of Science of Information.* New Delhi, Ess Ess Publication,2019.

DEWEY, John (1938): *Logic, the theory of enquiry,* New York, Henry Hall & Co, 1938.

DIKW Pyramid *en.m.wikipedia.org,*dated 25-04-2020.

DRIVER, Godfrey R. (1948), Semitic Writing from Pictograph to Alphabet, Oxford.

DRUCKER, Peter, F.(1969) *The Age of Discontinuity, Guidelines to Our Changing Society* ,Butterworth- Heinemann.

DRUCKER, Peter F. (1993), *Post-Capitalistic Society,* New York, Harper-Collins.

DUFF, Alistar S. (2000), *Information Society Studies,* London, Routeledge.

DURKHEIM, Emile (1919) *The Rules of Sociological Method and Selected Texts on Sociology and its Method* ed. by Steven Lukes, and tr. by W. D. Halls, New York, The Free Press (1895), Paris.

DYER, Christopher and GOLDSTEIN, Darwin (1970): *School libraries, theory and practice,* Bingley, 1970

EATON, J..J. and BAWDEN, D. (1991). "What kind of resource is information?". *International Journal of Information Management,* 11, P. 156-65

ELIOT, T.S.(1934), *Choruses from the Rock,* Poetry Nook, 1934

FAIRTHORNE, R. A.(1969), "Empirical Hyperbolic distribution (Bradford-Zipf Model lost) for bibliometric descrlption and prediction" *Journal of Documentation* 25:1969, p..319].

FAIRTHORNE, Robert A. (2005), "Empirical hyperbolic distributions for bibliometric distribution and prediction" *in Journal of Documentation* Vol. 61(2), January 2005, Pp.171-193.

FARHADPOOR, Mohammad Reza, (2017) *A study of Users' Motivation in using Information Services of Regional Information Center for Science and Technology,* Business.

FARRADANE, J. and MALCOM, G.(1962), "Education in Information Work: the syllabus and present curriculum of the Institute of Information Science, Ltd.", *Journal of Chemical Documentation,* Vol.2 (1962): pp.74-76.*fistsiteguide.com.*

FISHMAN, Stephen (2008): *The Copyright Handbook: What Every Writer Needs to Know,* Edn .10, Nolo, 2008; 527 p.

FREIDEN, J. et al (1998), "Information as a product, not goods, not services" *Marketing Intelligence & Planning* 3:1-13

GARFIELD, Eugene (1955). "Citation Indexes for Science: A New Dimension in Documentation through Association of ideas" *Science* 122 (3159), July 15,1955 Pp.108-111.

GARFIELD, Eugene (1971): "The mystery of the Transposed Journal Lists, wherein Bradford's Law of Scattering is generalized according to Garfield's Law of Concentration" *Current Contents,* 31 (1971): 5-6.

GODIN, Benoit (2008), "The Information Economy, the History of A Concept Through its Measurements 1949-2005" *The Project on the History and Sociology of S & T Statistics,* Working Paper No.18, 2008. Montreal, Canada.

GOFFMAN, W. and NEVILLE, V.A. (1964), "Communication and Epidemic Processes" *in Proceedings of the Royal Society of London, Series A: Mathematical and Physical Sciences,* Vol.298 No.1454 (May 2, 1967), Pp.316-334.

GOFFMAN, W. and NEVILLE, V.A. (1964) "A General Theory of Communication", ("Epidemic Theory of Communication; Epidemic model of the spread of scientific ideas as manifested by publication") *in* SARACEVIC, Tefko (1970), *Introduction to information Science,* Pp 726- , R.R. Bowker & Co, 1970.

GOFFMAN, W. and Warren, K.S. (1969) "Dispersion of papers among journals based on a mathematical analysis of two diverse medical literatures" *Nature* 221: 1205-1207.

GOFFMAN, W. and WARREN, K.S. (1980): *Scientific Information Systems and Principle of selectivity,* New York, Praeger

GRAY, John and PERRY, Brian, (1975), *Scientific Information* AGRIS, Information Systems Division, National Agricultural Library, Washington D.C.

GRIFFITH, et.al. (1979), "Ageing of scientific literature: a citation analysis" *Journal of Documentation* 35(179-196).

GUPTA, B.L. (1987) : *Knowledge , Communication and Library ,* Jaipur, Printwell, 1987.

GUPTA, DINESH k., (2010), "Marketing Library and Information Services" *in Encyclpaedia of Library and Information Sciences*, Edn.3, Taylor & Fraancis.

GUPTA, Sen I.N. (1973) "Recent growth of the literature of Biochemistry and changes in ranking of periodicals" *Journal of Documentation* 29 (2): 210-211.

HALDANE, J.B.S and HUXLEY, Julian (1927) *Animal Biology*, Oxford Clarendon, Google Scholar.

HARMON, Glynn (2008) "Remembering William Goffman: Mathematical Information Science Pioneer" *in Information Processing and Management, Vol* XXX (2008) (*www.sciencedirect.com*).

HOERULE, R F A (1952), *Studies in philosophy* ed by Daniel S. Robinson, London, A.G. Allen &Thomas, 1952.

HOLSTROM, J.E. 1962), *Aslib Proceedings* December 1962 .

HULME, E. Wyndham (1923), *Statistical Bibliography in relation to the growth of Modern civilization*, London, Butler & Turner Grafton.

IDRC, CANADA (1999), Marketing Information Products and Services; A Primer For Librarians And Information Professionals, ed by Abhinandan K. Jain, et al For Canada's International Development Research Centre.

INFOSCIENCE (2017). "Marketing information services; a conceptual framework", *Infoscience today*, November.*[http://www.infosciencetoday.org/type/articles/marketing-of-information-services-conceptual-_framework.html]*

INTERNATIONAL ENCYCLOPEDIA of Information Science (1997) ed. By John Feather and Paul Sturges.

IWINSKI, Boleslas (1911): "The Heritage of Boleslas Iwinski"S *in Library Trends* 62(2):456-464, September 2013.

JENNINGS, H.H.(1987) *Sociometry in Group Relations*, 2nd ed, Westport, Greenwood.

JESPERSON, Otto (1938), *Growth and structure of the English Language*, Rev Edn Read Books Ltd, 2011.

JESTIN.K.J. and PARAMESWARAN, R. (2002), "Marketing of Information Products and Services For Libraries In India" , *library Philosophy And Pratices* 5 (1), Fall.

JINHA, Arif E. "Article 50 million: an estimate of the number of scholarly articles in existence", *Learned Publishing* Vol. 23 No.4, July 2010.

JOHNSON, Elmer D. (1960). *Communication; an introduction to the history of the alphabet, writing, printing, books and libraries,* Edn.2. The Scarecrow Press, New York

JOHNSON, F. Craig and KLARE, G. R., "General models of communication research: a survey of the developments of a decade", *Journal of Communication,* 1961.

JOURNAL OF AMERICAN Society for Information Science (JASIS) (1974) 25:77-85.

KAWATRA, P. S. (1992), "Methods and Techniques of User Studies *in, Library user studies,* Bombay, Jaico Publ House,1992, Chapter 7, Pp.122-182.

KESSLER, M.M. (1963) "Bibliographic Coupling Between Scientific Papers", *American Documentation,* 14(1963):10-25.

KINCH, John W. *Ed.* (1971) *Sociology in the world of taday,* Massachusetts, Addison-Wesley Publishing Co.

KINGSMA, B. (1996), *The Economics Of Information,* Englewood, Libraries Unlimited.

KOCHEN, MANFRED (1964), *The Growth of Knowledge,* N.Y. John Wiley, 1964.

KOCHEN, Manfred (1983), "Information and Society" *ARIST* 18 (1983) pp.277-304.

KOHLER, Wolfgang (1947) , *Gestalt Psychology: An Introduction to New Concepts in Modern Psychology,* New york, Liveright.

KOTHARI, C.R. (2004) *Research Methodology, Methods and Techniques,* New Age International Publishers, Pp,10-19, 2004.

KOTLER, Philip (1986). "Megamarketing". ", *Harvard Business Review,* March-April 1986, P.116-124

KOTLER, Philip (2000). *Marketing management: the millennium edition,* (Edn.10), Prentice-Hall.

KUMAR, Manish and SINGH, Dr. K.P. (2015). "Marketing Of Library And Information Science Products And Services Through Social Media – Need Of The Hour", *Library Herald* , 53(4) December.

LAMBERTON, D.M. (1984), "The Economics of Information and Orgnisation" *in Annual Review of Information Science and Technology (ARIST),* 1984 (Vol 19), Pp. 4-30.

LASSWELL, Harold D (1948),"The Structure and Function of Communication in Society: the Communication of Ideas" New York, *Institute for Religious and Social Studies,*p.117.

LEIMKUHLER, F.F.(1967) "The Bradford Distribution", *Journal of Documentation,* 23(3) Pp.197-207.

LINE, M. B. (1970) "The half –life of periodical literature; apparent and real obsolescence", *Journal of Documentation* 26 (46-54).

LINE, M.B. and Sanderson, A. (1974), "Obsolescence and changes in the use of literature with time" *Journal of Documentation* 30:283-350.

LOTKA, Alfred J. (1926)"The frequency of distribution of scientific productivity" *Journal of the Washington Academy of Sciences* 16(12), 19 June1926 pp.317-323.

MACHLUP, Fritz (1962) *Production and Distribution of Knowledge in the United States,* Princeton University Press.

MALINOWSKI, Bronislaw (1929) The Sexual Life of Savages in North Western Menalesia, New York, Halcyon House.

MARSHAK, Jacob (1968) "Economics of Inquiring, Communicating, Deciding", American Economic Review, Vol 58 no.2, 1968 Pp.1-18.

MARX. Karl (1844), *Economic and Philosophic Manuscripts of 1844,* Moscow, Progress Publications, 1959.

McCARTHY, E. J. (1978). *Basic marketing ; a managerial approach* Edn. 6, Irwin Prentice-Hall

McLUHAN, Marshall (1964): *The Medium Is the Message: An Inventory of Effects,* Penguin Modern Classics.

MEAD, George Herbert (1934), *Mind, Self and Society,* The definitive Edition, University of Chicago Press.

MEADOWS, A.J. (1974), *Communication in Science, Butterworths*

MENZEL, Herbert (1966). "Information Needs and Uses in Science and Technology" in the *ARIST 1966.*

MEYER, MA. and ZACK, M.H. (1996), "The Design and Development Of Information Products", *Sloan Management Review, 43-59.*

MICHAEL, K. "History of Foundations of Information Science" *in Annual Review of Information Science and Technology* Vol. 12 (1977): 249-75.

MISHAN, E. J. (2007), *Cost-Benefit Analysis,* 5th edn, U.C. Berkley, Worth Publishers.

MORENO, Jacob L. (1934) *Who shall survive? A New approach to the Problem of Human Interrelations, Washington D.C.,*

Nervous and Mental Disease Publishing Co.

MORENO, Jacob L.(1943) "Sociometry and the Cultural Order", *Sociometry* 6:299-344.

NARAYANA MENON, V.K. (1976), *The Communication Revolution,* New Delhi, National Book Trust of India

NEISSER, Ulric (1967) *Cognitive Psychology,* Appleton- Century Crofts, 1967.

NYQUIST, Harry (1928) "Certain Topics In Telegraph Transmission Theory", *Trans. AAIEE,* Vol 47, pp 617-644, April 1928.

OGG, Oscar (1948), *The 26 Letters,* New York..

OLAISON, J.L. (1992), " Pricing Strategies For Library And Information Services": *in* Cronin, B. (ed): *The Marketing Of Library And Information Services,* London, Aslib, Pp. 238-78.

OSGOOD, Egerton and SCHRAMM , Wilbur(1954), "Osgood-Schramm Model of Communication: Definition and Application" *in Communication Models, Interpersonal Communication* (1954)

OTTEN, Klaus W. (1974), "Basis For A Science of Information" *in* Debons, A. *Ed. Information Science; Search for Identity,* New York, Marcel Dekker, 1974 pp.91-100.

PALMER, A. (2001). *Principles of service marketing,* Edn. E3. McGraw-Hill.

PARAMESWARAN, A. et al (1985). "A conceptual model of service quality and its implications for future research", *Journal of marketing,* Fall Page 41-59.

PARKER and PAISELEY *in* Tefko Saracevic: *Introduction to Information Science* Page 85-92.

PATIL, S.K. (2014), "Library Promotion Practices And Marketing Of Library Services; A Role of Library Profession", *Procedia Social And Behavioural Sciences* 133:249-254.

PORAT, Marc Uri (1977), *Information Economy; Sources and Methods for Measuring the Primary Information Sector (Detailed Industry* Reports), Washington D.C., U.S. Dept. of Commerce).

POTTER, W.G. (1981), "Introduction to Bibliometrics" *in Library Trends* 30:1981

PRICE, Derek, J. De Solla, (1963),*Little Science Big Science,* N.Y., Columbia University Press

PRICE, Derek J. de Solla, (1965), "Networks of Scientific Papers, the pattern of bibliographic references indicates the nature of the scientific research front", *Science*; 149 (3683), July 30, 1965 :510-515.

PRICE, Larry R. (2016), *Psychometric Methods: theory into Practice*, New York, Guilford Publications, 2016.

PRITCHARD, Alan (1969) "Statistical bibliography or bibliometrics?" *Journal of Documentation* 20(4) December 1969.

PUMPHREY, R.J. 91951), *The Origin of Language*, Liverpool...

RAGHAVIAH, Pushpa and AUGUSTINE , C. A. (1980), *Identification of the Core Literature in Information Science for the Master of Library & Information Science Programme and An Evaluation of the Kerala University Library Book Collection in the Area;* Dissertation submitted to the University of Kerala in partial fulfillment of the requirements of the Degree of Master of Library and Information Science, Department of Library & Information science, University of Kerala, Trivandrum, 1980.

RAISING, L. Miks. (1962), "Statistical bibliography in health sciences" *Bull of the Medical Library Association* 50:1962; pp.450-461.

RANGANATHAN,S. R. (1932), *Five Laws of Library Science,Madras Library Association*

RANGANATHAN, S.R. (1944), *Document Bibliography and Reference Service,* Madras Library Association.

RANGANATHAN, S.R. (1948) "Librametry"; concept presented at the ASLIB Conference held at Lemington Spa.

RATHSWOHL, Eugene J.(1972) "N*ature of information"*, in Debons, H. and Cameron, W.J. *Perspectives in Information Science,* Univ. of Pittsburgh, 1972,P. 21.

ROBBINS, Lionel (1935), *An Essay on the Nature and Significance of Economic Science*: London, Macmillan & Co.

ROWLEY, J.A. (2001), *Information marketing,* Ashgate Publishing

ROWLEY, Jennifer (2007) "The Wisdom hierarchy representations of the DIKW Hierarchy" *in Journal of Information and Communication Science,* 33(2):163-180.

ROWLEY,J.E. (1997) "Pricing And The Marketing Environment For Electronic Information" *Journal of Library And Information Science,* 29(2),Pp.95-102.

ROWLEY, J.E. and TURNER, G M D (1978), *The dissemination of information,* Boulder Co., Western Press, p. 298.

SARACEVIC, Tefko (1970), *Introduction to Information Science*, R.R. Bowker & Co. P.726.

SATYANARAYANA, N. R. (1966): *Information Technology and Its Facets*, New Delhi, Manal.

SATYANARAYANA, N.R and SATYANARAYANA, R. (1996): Problems of Information Science, New Age International,1996.

SAUNDERS, W.L. (1980), "Information the unscarce resources" *in The Proceedings of the Joint Conference of ASLIB, the Institute of Information Scientists and Library Association held in September 1980*, pages 1-12.

SCHRAMM, Wilbur (1972), 'How communication works' *in* K. J. McGrarry *Mass Communication, selected readings for librarians*. Linnet Books, 1972 P.17.

SHANNON, Claude E. (1948),"A Mathematical Theory of Communication" *The Bell System Technical; Journal*, 27(3):379-423, 1948.;

SHANNON, Claude E. and WEAVER, Warren (1949) *The Mathematical Theory of Communication* (1949), Chicao, University of Illinois Press.

SHARMA, A.K. and BHRADWAJ, S. A. (2009), "Marketing And Promotion Of Library Services", *Delhi University Library ICAL-2009 Advocacy And Marketing*

SHAW, Ralph R. (1956), *Pilot Study on the Use of Scientific Literature by Scientists*, Rutgers University, Dept of Library Science, 1956.

SHERA, Jesse H., *Foundations of Education for Librarianship*, N.Y. Wiley, Becker and Hayes, 1972 pp.164.

SIMON, Andrews (2000): "Information Science: Historical and Social Aspects, A World Outlook" *Journal of Documentation*, 56:p.12-14.

SMITH, Adam (1776) *An Enquiry into the Nature and Causes of the Wealth of Nations*, 2 Vols, W. Strahan T. Cadell, London.

SMITH, William and Vickers, I. (1973) "Sociometric Choice in Small Group Communication", *Journal of Applied Communication Research*, 1(2):97-103, Summer 1973.

SPENCE, A. Michael (1974), "An Economist's View of Information"in *ARIST 1974 (Vol.99)* Washington DC., American Society for Information Science.

STIGLER, G. J. (1961), "The Economics of Information", *Journal of Political Economy*, Vol. 69 Pp.213-25, 1961.

STIGLITZ, J.E. (2017), "Thee Revolution of Information Economics: the Past and the Future" NBER Working Paper No. 23780 issued in September 2017. National Bureau of Economics Research.

STRONG, William (1981): *The Copyright book*, MIT Press.

TANEJA, S.K. (1979), "Translation Services; Their Organisation and Documentation at National Level in India", *Annals of Library and Information Studies* Vol 26 (1-4): March –December, 1979.

THAYER, Lee (1963) "On Theory Building in Communication" *in Journal of Communication,* December 1963.

THAYER, LEE (1967), *Communication Concepts and Perspectives,* ERIC

TREADWELL, T. et. al. (1998) *Computerised Sociometry,* 2nd ed, Western Chlester University, PA.

TROSTINIKOV, V.N. (1926), "Information Science" *in Great Soviet Encyclopedia* Volume 10, PP. 274.

UNESCO (1981) *Many Voices One World (MacBride Commission Report); Communication and Society ; Today and Tomorrow,* Roman & Littlefield Publishers.

UNESCO (1981), *Many Voices One World, (MacBride Report); Towards a New More Just and More Efficient World Information and Communication Order,* Critical Media Studies.

VAN HOOUSE, Nancy A . (1984), "Research on the Economics of Libraries" *Library Trends,* 32(4), Pp. 407-423.

VERZOLA, Roberts (2004), *Towards A Political Economy of Information: Studies on the Information Economy,* Foundations of Nationalist /Studies, University of California,USA.

VICKERY, Alan and VICKERY, B.C. *(1987) Information Science in theory and practice, Butterworths, P.387.*

VICKERY, B.C. (1948) "Bradford's Law of scattering, *Journal of Documentation* 4 (3), PP.198-203.(1948).

WALLACE, Danny P. (2007) *Knowledge Management: Historical and Cross-Disciplinary Themes,* Libraries Unlimited, Pp.1-14.

WEBBER, S. (1993), "Charging For Information: Some Hints", *Inform* July-Aug: 3-4

WEBSTER, Frank (2O14), *Theories of the Information Society,* Edn.4, London, Routeledge.

WEISMAN, Charles M. (1985), *Strategic Information Systems,* McGraw-Hill Professional, 1985.

WEISS, Paul (1964): "Knowledge a growth process" *in* Manfred Kochen, Ed. *The growth of knowledge* N.Y., John Wiley,1964.

WHELDON, Harold J., *Wheldon's Cost Accounting and Costing Methods,* 13th Edn, by L.W.J. Owler and J..L. Brown, London, Macdonald & Evans, 1975.

WHITTENMORE, B. J. & YOVITS, M.C. (1972), *A Generalized Conceptual Development for the Analysis and Flow of Information,* Ohio State University, Computer and Information Science Research Center, 1972.

WHITTENMORE, Bruce J. and YOVITS, M.C. (1974): "The quantification and analysis of information used in decision processes" *in Information Sciences,* 7:171-184, December 1974.

WIENER, Norbert (1950) *The Human Use of Human beings; Cybernetics and Society* . Houghton Mifflin Harcourt, US.

WOOD, D.N. Ed. (1966), *Use of Earth Sciences literature,* Butterworth, London, 1966.

YANCEY, Rodney (2005): *Fifty Years of citation indexing and analysis,* Thompson scientific, 2005.

YUASA ,M. (1962), "Centre of Scientific Activity: its shift from the 16th to the 20th Century", *Japanese Studies in the History of Science,* No.1, 1962 Pp. 57-75.

ZACHERT & WILLIAMS (1992), Marketing Strategies for Information Services, Griffith

ZIPF, George Kingsley (1935). *The Psychobiology of Language,* Houghton-Mifflin.

ZIPF, George Kingsley (1949). *Human behavior and the Principles of Least Effort,* Cambridge Massachusetts, Addison Wesley.